T0295575

Management in the Non-Profit Sector

Despite the significant importance of the non-profit sector, there is a relative limitation of possible modeling related to the management of the Non-Profit Institutions (NPIs). The studies and the research are concentrated in the analysis of the characteristics and the limitations related to the NPIs, rather than to the identification of possible models that can guarantee virtuous paths to these organizations.

This book provides hypothetical trajectories for the construction of a theoretical model of reference for the management of NPIs—it accounts for the difficulties and the peculiarities of the non-profit sector, without however renouncing the concrete necessity and the great importance of approaches that try to avoid, or limit, the search for hybrid approaches constituted by the simple "transplant" of tools and techniques taken from the market or from the public administration context. Ultimately, it asserts that the non-profit sector is increasingly becoming the "pillar" on which modern civil society stands, to move toward a better future. The main aims of this book are to identify a link between accountability, responsibility and public trust in NPIs through a potential multidimensional managerial model in which these conceptual elements can be represented in a coordinated and systemic way.

It will be of interest to researchers, academics, policymakers and students in the fields of public and non-profit management, business management and administration, and public administration.

Renato Civitillo is a research fellow in the Department of Political Science at University of Naples Federico II, Italy.

Routledge Focus on Business and Management

The fields of business and management have grown exponentially as areas of research and education. This growth presents challenges for readers trying to keep up with the latest important insights. *Routledge Focus on Business and Management* presents small books on big topics and how they intersect with the world of business research.

Individually, each title in the series provides coverage of a key academic topic, whilst collectively, the series forms a comprehensive collection across the business disciplines.

Management in the Non-Profit Sector
A Necessary Balance Between Values, Responsibility and Accountability
Renato Civitillo

Fearless Leadership
Managing Fear, Leading with Courage and Strengthening Authenticity
Morten Novrup Henriksen and Thomas Lundby

Clusters, Digital Transformation and Regional Development in Germany
Marta Götz

Gender Bias in Organisations
From the Arts to Individualised Coaching
Gillian Danby and Malgorzata Ciesielska

For more information about this series, please visit: www.routledge.com/ Routledge-Focus-on-Business-and-Management/book-series/FBM

Management in the Non-Profit Sector

A Necessary Balance Between Values, Responsibility and Accountability

Renato Civitillo

NEW YORK AND LONDON

First published 2021
by Routledge
605 Third Avenue, New York, NY 10158

and by Routledge
2 Park Square, Milton Park, Abingdon, Oxon, OX14 4RN

Routledge is an imprint of the Taylor & Francis Group, an informa business

© 2021 Taylor & Francis

The right of Renato Civitillo to be identified as author of this work
has been asserted by him in accordance with sections 77 and 78 of the
Copyright, Designs and Patents Act 1988.

Library of Congress Cataloging-in-Publication Data
Names: Civitillo, Renato, 1982- author.
Title: Management in the non-profit sector : a necessary balance
    between values, responsibility and accountability / Renato
    Civitillo.
Description: 1 Edition. | New York : Routledge, 2021. | Series:
    Routledge focus on business and management | Includes
    bibliographical references and index.
Identifiers: LCCN 2020057536 (print) | LCCN 2020057537
    (ebook) | ISBN 9780367256586 (hardback) | ISBN
    9780429290183 (ebook)
Subjects: LCSH: Nonprofit organizations—Management. | Values. |
    Social responsibility of business.
Classification: LCC HD62.6 .C528 2021 (print) | LCC HD62.6
    (ebook) | DDC 658/.048—dc23
LC record available at https://lccn.loc.gov/2020057536
LC ebook record available at https://lccn.loc.gov/2020057537

ISBN: 978-0-367-25658-6 (hbk)
ISBN: 978-1-032-02238-3 (pbk)
ISBN: 978-0-429-29018-3 (ebk)

Typeset in Times New Roman
by Apex CoVantage, LLC

To my beloved daughter, Camilla, and to my wife, Pina, the love of my life.

To my parents, Ida and Raffaele, for always loving and supporting me.

Contents

Tables

Figures

Acknowledgment

This book was born from the idea of extending to the international context the studies and investigations relating to the non-profit sector initially developed by the author with reference only to the Italian context. For this reason, the considerations it collects are the result of scientific research and observations settled over a rather long period of time, and which involved various people.

I am personally grateful to each of the people with whom I have had the honor and the pleasure of discussing such a complex and articulated issue as the one underlying the book. However, my first and biggest thank you is to Professor Paolo Ricci, for his continuous supervision and mentoring, which began many years ago and, fortunately for me, is still present every day.

The book has undergone a rigorous review process: therefore, a special thanks goes to the reviewers, whose patience and dedication have ensured the book's highest quality level.

Finally, I would like to thank my publisher Routledge of the Taylor and Francis Group, and, in particular, Brianna Ascher (Editor for business and management disciplines) and Naomi Round Cahalin (Editorial Assistant): their support was crucial throughout the book writing process.

Preface

In 1989, Peter Drucker wrote:

> Twenty years ago, management was a dirty word for those involved in nonprofit organizations. It meant business, and nonprofits prided themselves on being free of the taint of commercialism and above such sordid considerations as the bottom line. Now most of them have learned that nonprofits need management even more than business does, precisely because they lack the discipline of the bottom line.
>
> (p. 89)

Since that time, almost 30 years ago, much has changed on the subject of Non-Profit, and Non-Profit Institutions (NPIs), especially concerning:

- Their nature,
- Their functions,
- Their management models.

The Non-Profit Institutions' need for managerial techniques inevitably clash with the absence of traditional for-profit price mechanisms, creating important potential confusions (Moore, 2000) and leading to an "overload" of managerial schemes (Skelcher & Smith, 2015).

The non-profit sector includes a wide range of organizations with really very varied characteristics. Just to give some examples: museums; schools and universities; research institutes; health, banking and credit organizations; environmental associations; humanitarian organizations; religious bodies; sports and recreational associations and many others.

However, this summary list shows that Non-Profit Institutions, as a whole, seem to represent the "pillars" on which modern civil society stands (Anheier, 2014).

Consequently, it is not difficult to understand that the importance expressed by the non-profit sector has progressively and inexorably grown so much that, nowadays, it represents an indispensable reference point for citizens in almost all the countries of the world.

In this sense, nowadays, the Non-Profit is so complex, multifaceted and articulated to represent one of the main actors in the supply and provision of certain categories of goods and services, as well as being one of the main employers of a very high number of workers (Salamon & Anheier, 1996).

Consequently, this means that the awareness and the need for a more managerialism for non-profit sector are considerably increased. Given the role of Non-Profit Institutions (as just highlighted), it is undeniable that the related governance models and management must necessarily be based on levels of efficiency and effectiveness that can guarantee that the functioning of these organizations can ensure the supply of those goods and services which are, in many cases, of vital importance for the communities and citizens.

Non-Profit Institutions, in effect, could be considered as the direct result of civil society as they are able to improve government effectiveness and ensure higher levels of economic development and community satisfaction: some scholars (Putnam, 2001) claim that the value of Non-Profit Institutions consists precisely in:

• Their ability to support and promote their communities;
• Their role in promoting and sustaining the commitment of local communities and their citizens;
• The creation of networks to exchange information from/to the resident population and, in general, extensive forms of social and professional networking.

In other words, Non-Profit Institutions have to do with "civic-engagement objectives": unlike for-profit institutions, the economic object of Non-Profit Institutions must necessarily be combined with the aim of satisfying the needs of the civic communities and of the citizens who are part of it. This makes it very complex:

• Their management (and necessary activities), and
• The correct reporting and demonstration of the value that they are able to generate.

Despite the significant importance of the non-profit sector, we can note a relative limitation of possible modeling related to the management of Non-Profit Institutions. In other words, the studies and the research are more concentrated in the analysis of the characteristics and the limitations related to Non-Profit Institutions rather than to the identification of possible models that can guarantee virtuous paths to these organizations.

This book tries to provide some hypothetical trajectories for the construction of a theoretical model of reference for the management of Non-Profit Institutions: this model tries to account for the difficulties and the peculiarities of the Non-Profit Sector, without however renouncing the concrete necessity and the great importance of approaches that try to avoid, or at least limit, the search for hybrid approaches constituted by the simple "transplant" of tools and techniques taken from the market or from the public administration context.

It follows a three-dimensional scheme, based on three key elements:

1. Values,
2. Accountability, and
3. Managerialism.

References

Anheier, H. K. 2014. *Nonprofit Organizations: Theory, Management, Policy*, second edition. New York: Routledge.

Moore, M. H. 2000. Managing for value: Organizational strategy in for-profit, nonprofit, and governmental organizations. *Nonprofit and Voluntary Sector Quarterly*, 29(1), 183–204.

Putnam, R. D. 2001. *Bowling Alone: The Collapse and Revival of American Community*. New York: Simon and Schuster.

Salamon, L. M., & Anheier, H. K. 1996. *The International Classification of Nonprofit Organizations: ICNPO-Revision 1*. Baltimore, MD: Johns Hopkins University Institute for Policy Studies.

Skelcher, C., & Smith, S. R. 2015. Theorizing hybridity: Institutional logics, complex organizations, and actor identities: The case of nonprofits. *Public Administration*, 93(2), 433–448.

1 Introduction

Summary

This chapter deals with Non-Profit topic, which undoubtedly represents a phenomenon of difficult interpretation and treatment. These difficulties can already be found in the same definition of the concept: it, in fact, lends itself to being somewhat ambiguous, blurred and equivocal, in both virtue and the vagueness of its use in common language, and especially in consideration of its application to the empirical reality, which today consists of innumerable and varied organizational forms traditionally made to fall within this complex term.

First of all, we need to highlight the residual use of the not-for-profit concept, which is generally used to indicate any form of organization with which citizens act on the public stage. In this perspective, we could theoretically distinguish two different forms of non-profit:

- *A form that we could define "healthy",*
- *A category that we could call, on the contrary, "pathological".*

The "healthy" form of non-profit coincides with the set of organizations whose mission is to provide a wide range of services and products to citizens and communities (Frumkin & Andre-Clark, 2000; Moore, 1995, 2000): this is the reason that justifies the particular protection regime present in many legal systems. In other terms, Non-Profit Institutions, very often, can benefit from particularly favorable tax treatment, through a preferential regime based precisely on the particular social and welfare purposes of these organizations. In the Unites States, for example, the Government provides supply-side tax subsidies related to specific forms of charity (Brody & Cordes, 2006). In addition, individuals and corporations can deduct the value of charitable contributions against income and estate taxes and against the taxable value or estates.

On the opposite end of this continuum, instead, we find the form that we could define as "pathological non-profit" to refer to the aggregative forms aimed exclusively at the enjoyment of favorable measures (above all of fiscal, as well as competitive, labor law and of another kind) and therefore lacking the actual canons of social utility which, instead, should represent their founding presuppositions. For example, in the Unites States, non-profits can lose their tax exemption or face penalties called "intermediate sanctions" if they do not respect some rules: according to IRS, the revenue service of the United States federal government, tens of thousands of non-profit organizations have their tax-exempt status revoked every year.

On this point, it is really necessary to note how the "deviated" forms of non-profit sector do not constitute mere and simple distortions of the original associative phenomenon, but rather manifestations of intrinsic characteristics of the same.

1.1 The Non-Profit Phenomenon

The non-profit sector can be defined as the set of private, voluntary and non-profit organizations and associations (Anheier, 2014), through which citizens and communities can act for the protection of a general public interest.

The term non-profit sector is also defined as "third sector" to underline its peculiar intermediate position between government and public administration, on the one hand, and business or private for-profit market, on the other.

The term, therefore, refers both to a theoretical concept and also to a sector that has recently acquired ever greater importance.

Furthermore, it is a concept that does not have perfectly defined boundaries and, above all, unchangeable over time. On the contrary, some authors (DiMaggio & Anheier, 1990; Salamon et al., 1999; Anheier, 2000, 2014) clearly highlight that, in modern economic systems, the non-profit sector tends to present a rather fluid and nuanced perimeter, with organizational realities that often pass with enormous ease from one category to the other (e.g., some initially public hospitals become non-profit, and then come to organizational forms of a profit-oriented type).

On the other hand, some Non-Profit Institutions have particularly intense and close relationships with public government authorities and with profit-oriented organizations through, for example, specific programs or projects: in these cases, as in many others, it becomes really difficult or misleading to exclusively qualify such contexts such as Non-Profit Institutions (LeRoux & Feeney, 2015).

Another term commonly used as a synonym for non-profit sector is that of "voluntary sector" or "volunteering", traditionally used to highlight the voluntary character of the people commonly involved in this type of entity. However, even in this case, it is a term that can lend itself to misinterpretations, when these tend to a high degree of generalization. In fact, the

empirical reality presents many organizations whose staff are highly profes-
sionalized but, above all, fairly and physiologically paid.

1.2 "Healthy" and "Pathological" Forms of Non-Profit Institutions

The non-profit phenomenon undoubtedly represents a logical category that
is difficult to deal with (Fiorentini, 1997; Barbetta, Cima & Zamaro, 2003;
Anheier, 2000; Bronzetti, 2007; Anheier, 2014). The interpretative difficulties can be found in the definition of the concept itself: in fact, it lends itself
to being somewhat elusive by virtue of both the vagueness of its use in
common language, (and more) in consideration of its application to empirical reality, which consists of today of innumerable and variegated organizational forms traditionally included in this term.

In fact, it is not at all difficult to imagine the substantially residual use
of the concept of non-profit, generally designed to indicate any form of
organization with which citizens act on the public scene. However, this
conceptualization also represents the "healthy" form of non-profit, such as
to justify the particular protection regime present in our legal system. On
the opposite extreme of this continuum is the form that we could define as
"pathological" of the non-profit sector, if it refers to the aggregative forms
aimed exclusively at the enjoyment of the tax incentives (especially of a
fiscal nature, as well as competition, labor law and other types) and therefore lacking the effective canons of social utility which, instead, should
represent their founding assumptions. On this point, it is really necessary
to note how different authors (Moro, 2014) are who believe that the "deviated" forms of non-profit do not constitute mere and simple distortions of
the original associative phenomenon, but rather manifestations of intrinsic
characteristics of the same. This critical reflection is by no means insignifi-
cant; on the contrary, it probably allows us to highlight the crucial point of
the question: the correct conceptualization of non-profit.

With regard to the second aspect, the theme is once again connected to
the definitional question. In this sense, it should be borne in mind that, in
some countries the primordial roots of the non-profit phenomenon can be
traced back to the Middle Ages: it is in this period that works and congrega-
tions of charity, religious and lay people who use the huge resources at their
disposal to guarantee the support of the weakest people or, in general, for
interests belonging to the community. Nonetheless, the official recognition
of the central role of forms of associations aimed at protecting social needs
can only be obtained with the approval of the Constitutions of some countries where this sensitivity was deemed relevant by the people involved in
the respective constitutional foundation: it is the inclusion of the Non-Profit

Institutions in the Constitutions that decrees the formal birth of the "non-profit sector," which is thus defined as the set of all organizational forms having a social purpose aimed at guaranteeing the collective and subsidiary needs of the institutions typically state-owned.

While considering the necessary and obvious differences between the various countries (Salamon & Anheier, 1992, 1996; Salamon, 1999; Anheier, 2014; LeRoux & Feeney, 2015; Skelcher & Smith, 2015), we can highlight that the non-profit phenomenon has undergone a complex evolution which, essentially, can be divided into four main periods:

1. 1970s–1980s: the pioneering period.

   It is the period in which the non-profit sector is oriented toward the search for solutions to needs generally not guaranteed by the public sector. Consequently, it finds substance mainly through Catholic charitable associations committed to particular categories of people considered disadvantaged (such as drug addicts and disabled people) which represent a sort of response to the revolutionary movements of 1968. Furthermore, in this phase, in the various countries the first legislative interventions aimed at defining the characteristics of the Non-Profit Institutions are beginning to be approved.

2. 1990s: the expansion and organizational consolidation.

   The non-profit sector, after the embryonic phase of a self-organizational type, undergoes an evident dimensional development that requires a greater commitment at the organizational level. This phase is also characterized by many regulatory measures that continue to define, in an increasingly analytical way, the peculiarities of the non-profit sector and its organizations.

3. 2000s: the institutionalization period.

   The significant growth and expansion recorded in previous periods pose, with the beginning of the new millennium, an evident need for the institutionalization of the non-profit phenomenon. For this reason, this phase is particularly important and delicate because Non-Profit Institutions are beginning to be given the fundamental leading role in the design and planning of local social services in various countries.

4. From 2000 to today: the complexification period.

   The continuous and progressive progress of the expansion phase requires, in addition to the institutionalization of the previous phase, greater attention to the organizational aspects of non-profit institutions which become the necessary support for the correct and rational management of increasingly composite, multiform and heterogeneous structures. It is in this phase that Non-Profit Institutions begin to assume increasingly complex organizational characteristics, becoming extremely articulated and complex organizations, due to the need to give adequate response to the growing needs of modern civil society.

The synthetic reconstruction of the main historical phases characterizing the "non-profit" phenomenon cannot neglect the observation of the extreme difficulty in identifying a universally shared definition of a "non-profit sector" even if, on the other hand, there have been several scientific attempts to initiate in-depth and specific studies on the subject. In this sense, an essential point of reference is represented by the definition elaborated in the course of the extensive international survey curated, since 1990, by Johns Hopkins University and promoted by the University of Baltimore. At the helm of the aforementioned project, in 1996, scholars Lester Salamon and Helmut Anheier, in order to systematically collect information on the non-profit sector, conducted a comparative research between 13 countries, including Italy, drawing inspiration precisely from the need to guarantee a correct framing of the non-profit sector through a general reconfiguration of social and economic life which, up to that moment, was anchored to the ideal presence of only two actors: the Government and the private market. In other words, such a conceptual approach did not consider the existence of "private" organizations in form, but having purposes substantially pertaining to the public sphere. For this reason, the research was set precisely in the direction of giving these organizations the right economic and social weight: the goal, however, can only be pursued by passing through an orthodox categorization of organizations falling into the logical category of the non-profit sector.

From what has been explained up to now, it is quite evident how the non-profit phenomenon is characterized by various limits and criticalities and which essentially concern the very conceptual construction of the non-profit. According to some scholars (Anheier, 2000, 2014; Boris & Steuerle, 2017), the fundamental weaknesses could be classified into three fundamental types:

• Defining limits,
• General limits, and
• Technical, methodological and scientific limits.

The defining limits essentially concern the generalized tendency to the residual construction of subjects (and objects) to be included in the non-profit sector. In other words, the non-profit phenomenon has always been negatively reconstructed, starting from the definition of what it does not represent or, also, what it should not represent. Such an approach, evidently, is absolutely not consistent with the importance represented by the non-profit sector, both in Italy and internationally.

The general limits, on the other hand, concern first and foremost the absolute prevalence of the economic aspect in the treatment of the non-profit phenomenon which, too often, is abandoned to an isolated evaluation limited to this (single) dimension. The consideration of the non-profit sector only in its employment, income, or other quantitative economic aspects determines a series of absolutely negative consequences, as it makes marginal activities not directly aimed at the production of goods and services (e.g., protection of citizens' rights, protection of environment, protection of the disabled).

Finally, the technical, methodological and scientific limits are still partly connected with the definition problem already mentioned earlier. In fact, analyzing the entire non-profit sector, it is possible to find quite varied and distinct realities. In the classification of non-profit organizations, entities with different characteristics and peculiarities can coexist, with deeply heterogeneous purposes and, in some cases, very distant from each other. The inclusion in a single logical container of this vast and differentiated panorama of subjects should lead to realities that are an expression of the same phenomenology and that, therefore, should be treated in the same way. In this perspective, Table 1.1 provides only some typical examples of organizations that, in modern civil society, can be constituted in the form of Non-Profit Institution. It is evident, however, that from a simple reading of the various types of organizations typically included in the non-profit sector, we perceive a heterogeneity that is too high to be referred to a homogeneous phenomenon.

To the issues briefly outlined so far, we then add the theme of the correct connotation of the non-profit sector. This aspect is linked to the positive effect generated by some types of activities (and, therefore, organizations) toward all those included in the vast and heterogeneous logical container described earlier. In short, the positive image of part of the realities that are part of the non-profit is in fact reverberated on the whole that, therefore, benefits from the merit, gratitude and social utility produced by a (very often limited) part of the whole reference universe. In this direction, for example, volunteering and its emblematic and typical expression of response to the daily needs of social justice and solidarity has, in fact, given representation to the entire non-profit sector, so much so that it also generates a mixture of terminology between volunteering and non-profit, with the first paradoxically absorbing the second.

Table 1.1 Some typical examples of Non-Profit Institutions

Museums	Foundations
Orchestras	Service organizations
Schools	Fraternities and sororities
Universities	Special interest associations and advocacy groups
Adult education	Self-help groups
Research institutions	Sports and recreations clubs
Policy think-tank	Political parties
Health	Philanthropic organizations and charities
Mental health	Trade Unions
Human services	Non-Governmental Organizations (NGOs)
Credit and savings	Sports federations and associations
Environment and natural resources	Religious associations
Local development and housing	Agricultural associations
Humanitarian relief associations and international development organizations	Artistic and cultural associations
Human rights organizations	Environmental associations
Rural farmers' associations	Recreational associations
Religious associations	Military associations

Source: Author elaboration.

All this allows us to highlight some more reflections.

First of all, we can realize the extreme complexity of the phenomenon analyzed. This complexity, therefore, is also the basis of the critical issues outlined earlier. Therefore, a first aspect that should be emphasized concerns the fact that the (complex) phenomenon of non-profit cannot be tackled by relegating it to the "specialisms" of professionals (Civitillo, 2016). The topic, on the other hand, should be the subject of extensive discussions and be able to guarantee the involvement of a large part of the public which, in light of the characteristics of the non-profit sector, can be seen as its true reference subject. On the other hand, often, the non-profit phenomenon has been tackled with excessive specialisms (normative or cognitive) that have seen the integrated and systemic vision so necessary fail.

From the previous observation, then, a second observation follows: the criticalities of the non-profit do not represent a pathological degeneration, but an externalization of elements of fragility that have always existed and that, therefore, pervade the phenomenon in an intrinsic way.

For what has been said, therefore, it can be highlighted that the fundamental hub of the non-profit phenomenon is represented by the identification of social utility attributable to the organizations that are part of it. This utility can only be represented exclusively by the activities that the organizations themselves provide. From this, it follows that the identification criterion of the social value (Putnam, 2001; Porter & Kramer, 2011) is represented by the proximity of the promoted activities with respect to the general interest, with the latter declinable with respect to at least three meanings:

1. The general interest deriving from the Constitution and the laws;
2. The general interest arising from international declarations and documents concerning human rights; and
3. The general interest deriving from the reference political community.

The centrality of the general interest, in the reference role of a possible evaluation of the social utility of non-profit activities, is clearly evident if we think of the simple observation that the birth of a community is directly connected to the identification of one or more specific interests able to unite its members (Ricci, 2010). Consequently, the provision of public services represents one of the most characteristic activities for the well-being and serenity of the community itself: in this sense, we may argue that every time a service is public it means that it has been deemed worthy of a general interest, of an interest that the community puts above everything, above every member of the same community. In other words, reasoning in a specular way, the presence of a public service necessarily postulates and requires the presence of a common good which, in turn, can be represented by the realization of the social and moral progress of a community or by the achievement of satisfactory and satisfying living conditions of the members themselves. In summary, therefore, it could be emphasized that the concept of general interest refers to all the activities of public institutions and the consequent contribution they make to the interest of the community as a whole, as well as to that of specific groups or that of single individuals. The transversal character of the public interest thus implies the need for a synthesis between different expectations, for example, between people of different ages or with different religious, ethical or moral values. Naturally, what has just been reported must necessarily be contextualized to the non-profit sector, due to the fact that Non-Profit Institutions differ from institutions of public origin precisely because the former are characterized by more specific interests than the latter, according to which processes are implemented of voluntary aggregation of the subjects animated by their pursuit. The clarification, however, does not limit the scope of what was previously observed: it is the general interest that represents the main benchmark for any analysis of the social value of the non-profit sector.

In general, it is believed that the entire non-profit sector has been conceptually built on the United States welfare model, which is completely different from the typical European one, especially in terms of the role of the state in the management of these activities. Indeed, in the typical United States system, much of the education, social, health, retirement and retirement benefits are provided by the community, not the state. This system is supported by tax-exemption policies for economic contributions to (nonpublic) organizations that provide these services. In the European model, on the other hand, it is the state that assumes the role of a guarantor of the wellbeing of citizens. Consequently, the non-profit sector has found its concrete explanation in the crisis of the welfare state and, therefore, in the connected need to identify a subjectivity capable of ensuring—both in a position of support and as a substitute—a varied range of services: according to this vision, the non-profit sector could be configured as a multifaceted instrument for formalizing and externalizing private-sector entrepreneurial initiatives for the provision of various services requested by the community. These different peculiarities, therefore, create a situation of evident differentiation that does not reconcile with a "universal" logical categorization of the non-profit phenomenon and which, on the other hand, would require different and specific cultural or legislative guidelines depending on the specific context considered. Unfortunately, however, this was not the case and, often, there is a tendency to impose transversal logics on the non-profit sector that do not consider at all the specific characteristics of the specific representations of certain contexts.

References

Anheier, H. K. 2014. *Nonprofit Organizations: Theory, Management, Policy*, second edition. New York: Routledge.

Anheier, H. K. 2000. Managing non-profit organisations: Towards a new approach. *Civil Society Working Paper 1*. London: Centre for Civil Society, LSE.

Barbetta, G. P., Cima, S., & Zamaro, N. 2003. *Le istituzioni Nonprofit in Italia*. Bologna: Il Mulino.

Boris, E. T., & Steuerle, C. E. (Eds.) 2017. *Nonprofits & Government: Collaboration & Conflict*. Washington, DC: The Urban Institute.

Brody, E., & Cordes, J. J. 2006. Tax treatment of nonprofit organizations: A two-edged sword? In Boris, E. T., & Steuerle, C. E. (Eds.), *Nonprofits & Government: Collaboration & Conflict*. Washington, DC: The Urban Institute.

Bronzetti, G. 2007. *Le aziende Non Profit*. Milano: FrancoAngeli.

Civitillo, R. 2016. *L'aziendalità nel volontariato. Il non profit nella provincia di Benevento*. Milano: FrancoAngeli.

DiMaggio, P., & Anheier, H. K. 1990. A sociological conceptualization of the nonprofit organizations and sectors. *Annual Review of Sociology*, 16, 137–159.

Fiorentini, G. 1997. *Organizzazioni non profit e di volontariato*. Direzione, marketing e raccolta fondi. Etas, Milano.

Frumkin, P., & Andre-Clark, A. 2000. When mission, markets and politics collide: Values and strategy in the nonprofit human services. *Nonprofit and Voluntary Sector Quarterly*, 29(1), 141–163.

LeRoux, K., & Feeney, M. K. 2015. *Nonprofit Organizations and Civil Society in the United States*. New York: Routledge.

Moore, M. H. 2000. Managing for value: Organizational strategy in for-profit, nonprofit, and governmental organizations. *Nonprofit and Voluntary Sector Quarterly*, 29(1), 183–204.

Moore, M. H. 1995. *Creating Public Value: Strategic Management in Government*. Cambridge, MA: Harvard University Press.

Moro, G. 2014. *Contro il Non Profit*. Bari: Laterza.

Porter, M. E., & Kramer, M. R. 2011. The big idea: Creating shared value. *Harvard Business Review*, 89(1), 2.

Putnam, R. D. 2001. *Bowling Alone: The Collapse and Revival of American Community*. New York: Simon and Schuster.

Ricci, P. 2010. *Il soggetto economico nell'azienda pubblica*. Un'introduzione su chi comanda davvero nell'azienda pubblica e perché. RIREA, Roma.

Salamon, L. M. (Ed.) 1999. *Global Civil Society, Volume One: Dimensions of the Nonprofit Sector*. Baltimore, MD: The Johns Hopkins Center for Civil Society Studies.

Salamon, L. M., & Anheier, H. K. 1996. *The International Classification of Nonprofit Organizations: ICNPO-Revision 1*. Baltimore, MD: Johns Hopkins University Institute for Policy Studies.

Salamon, L. M., & Anheier, H. K. 1992. In search of the nonprofit sector II: The question of classification. *Voluntas*, 3(3), 267–309.

Salamon, L. M., Anheier, H. K., List, R., Toepler, S., Sokolowski, S. W., & Associates 1999. *Global Civil Society: Dimensions of the Non-Profit Sector*. Baltimore, MD: Johns Hopkins University Institute for Policy Studies.

Skelcher, C., & Smith, S. R. 2015. Theorizing hybridity: Institutional logics, complex organizations, and actor identities: The case of nonprofits. *Public Administration*, 93(2), 433–448.

2 The Non-Profit Sector and Its Institutions

Summary

The second chapter tries to address the following primary question: why do Non-Profit Institutions exist?

To find the most useful answers to the aforementioned question, this chapter leads the reader between the concepts of pure public goods, pure private goods and the so-called "quasi-public goods" (Samuelson, 1954;Musgrave, 1959;Buchanan, 1968). In fact, mainstream economic theory (Rosen, 2004) states that each one of main economic actors—market, Government and Non-Profit Institutions—is more suitable and specialized in providing a particular category of goods and services:

- *The market should best supply pure private goods and services,*
- *The Government should be more appropriate in providing pure public goods and services, and*
- *Non-Profit Institutions would have the natural role (at least prominently) to take care of quasi-public goods and services.*

In other words, Non-Profit Institutions' existence would be explained by what are called "failures" situations.

In this perspective, the explanation of why Non-Profit Institutions exist lies in many theories most of which are relatively recent (DiMaggio & Anheier, 1990; Ben-Ner & Gui, 1993;Hansmann, 1996;Rose-Ackerman, 1996;Salamon, 1999), like the Trust-related theories (Arrow, 1963;Hansmann, 1987;Ortmann & Schlesinger, 2003) or the Entrepreneurship theories (James, 1987;Rose-Ackerman, 1996; Dees, Emerson & Economy, 2001) but, in general, all of them seem to pose a crucial question: whether market economies are aimed at profit, why are there some organizations that decide not to foresee profit as a priority of their system of values?

Trying to answer this question, we need to point out that:

1) *Non-Profit Institutions are "Non-Profit-distributing" organizations (although, not "Non-Profit-making") (Anheier, 2014).*
2) *They are built on a very deep value system which necessarily influences their organization and performance.*

These two features imply that Non-Profit Institutions appear to be organizational entities that must coexist in a particularly complex and delicate conceptual space, that is intermediate between business and public government; their value system implies a very complex performance behavior because the achievement of their goals is conditioned by values pursued within their mission and vision (Moore, 1995; Najam, 1996; Speckbacher, 2003; Toepler & Anheier, 2004; Porter & Kramer, 2011): politics, religion, ethics, voluntarism, philanthropy and compassion are just some examples.

2.1 Why Do Non-Profit Institutions Exist?

In the international scientific literature, it is possible to identify various theories that, albeit according to very varied methodologies and purposes, have tried to explain the existence of Non-Profit Institutions and the needs that would justify their continuous development (DiMaggio & Anheier, 1990; Hansmann, 1996; Rose-Ackerman, 1996; Salamon et al., 1999). However, these theories, despite being characterized by very different approaches, seem to be built and based on a common and very crucial question: why do Non-Profit Institutions exist?

In other words, because market economies are generally oriented to profit, if any organization decides not to be profit-making, we should expect one or more reasons to justify their existence and their subsequent success.

In this sense, the mainstream economic theory (Rosen, 2004) states that each one of main economic actors—market, Government and Non-Profit Institutions—is more suitable and specialized in providing a particular category of goods and services:

- Market should best supply pure private goods and services.
- Government should be more appropriate with reference to pure public goods and services.
- Non-Profit Institutions would have the natural role (at least prominently) to take care of quasi-public goods and services.

Trying to answer the aforementioned question, we need to point out that:

1. Non-Profit Institutions are "non-profit-distributing" organizations (although, not "non-profit-making") (Anheier, 2014, p. 196).

2. They are built on a very deep value system that necessarily influences their organization and performance.

First of all, it is very interesting to highlight that Non-Profit Institutions could (or probably should) be more correctly considered as "non-profit-distributing" organizations rather than as "non-profit-making" entities (Anheier, 2014), mainly because Non-Profit Institutions are structurally conceived as economic organizations in which incoming monetary flows are destined for the exercise of their institutional activities and, therefore, for their mission; on the other hand, it is not envisaged that incoming resources can be distributed, in any way, to the various governing bodies of the same organizations.

All this means that any financial resources generated by the operation of this particular type of organization are mainly reinvested or otherwise allocated to the declared mission of the organization.

This would lead to the following conclusions:

1. Non-Profit Institutions, unlike private for-profit organizations, are unrelated to the generation of profits or, in general, of positive financial differences.
2. The acquisition of resources (financial and otherwise) in Non-Profit Institution is very sensitive to levels of efficiency and effectiveness in the pursuit of the aforementioned institutional needs, with evident management consequences.

Furthermore, it is particularly useful to highlight that the management of Non-Profit Institutions can never allow the abandonment of the basic economic patterns typical of any economic organization, regardless of whether it is of the "profit" or "non-profit" type. In both cases, the processes and management schemes are substantially similar, diverging only in aspects related to specific purposes: "profit" or "non-profit" objectives (Civitillo, 2016).

The preceding text seems to highlight that Non-Profit Institutions are organizational entities that must coexist in a conceptual space that is intermediate between business and public government; their value system implies a very complex performance behavior because the achievement of their goals is conditioned by values pursued within their mission and vision (Najam, 1996; Speckbacher, 2003; Toepler & Anheier, 2004; Smith, 2010): politics, religion, ethics, voluntarism, philanthropy, giving, compassion, civil society, charity, civic engagement and social capital are just some example.

2.2 Non-Profit Between "Values" and "Value"

Some authors (Moore, 2000; Smith, 2008) argue that Non-Profit Institutions have a link with their value system that is so close that even these organizations identify the activities to be carried out without considering the potential economic-financial profitability but, contrary:

- The compliance of the activities with respect to its mission,
- The compatibility of the activities with respect to the institutionally pursued values, and
- The possibility of ensuring an efficient process of creating global value.

In this sense, therefore, a particularly important role is represented by the mission which, therefore, becomes a fundamental element for the Non-Profit Institutions as it is able to define the value of the organization itself for the community, as well as a decisive tool for both evaluation and the performance of Non-Profit Institutions, and as a strategic planning tool for their future development.

These considerations allow us to understand that in Non-Profit Institutions there is a sort of mixture between "values" and "value": this relationship is no longer negligible and deeply conditions the approaches, principles, tools and operating methods by evaluating the Non-Profit Institutions.

In this perspective, we must remember that, although the management of any economic organization necessarily requires performance evaluation processes, this varies considerably according to the type of organization considered:

- In the purposes pursued,
- In the operating modes to be used.

In this perspective, the non-profit sector constitutes a very particular area of economic organizations, because it is characterized by three peculiarities (Anheier, 2000; Civitillo, 2016):

1. The absence of profit,
2. The difficulty of using reliable financial parameters and criteria, and
3. The mission is strongly influenced by the set of values pursued with its activities.

These elements determine that Non-Profit Institutions are commonly defined as "hybrid" organizations and this "hybridity" makes it very difficult to identify the most useful criteria and tools for the correct management and evaluation of these entities (Billis, 2010; Battilana et al., 2012; Battilana & Lee, 2014).

Furthermore, considering that, as mentioned earlier, profit is not the main management element in Non-Profit Institutions (as happens in profit-oriented organizations); a further consequence is that the performance evaluation in these particular entities is extremely ambiguous, even a function of that system of values mentioned previously, and which is vast, unclear, vague, imprecise, heterogeneous and difficult to express with quantitative measures. Despite this, the Non-Profit Institution value system influences the set of planned objectives and the ways in which these are achieved (Najam, 1996; Porter & Kramer, 1999; Moore, 2000; Putnam, 2001; Speckbacher, 2003; Toepler & Anheier, 2004).

2.3 Main Features of Non-Profit Institutions

What has just been stated leads to the need to seek an institutional approach in the treatment of this book and which, therefore, concerns the institutes, the entities that can qualify as non-profit. By virtue of such an approach we can disregard the general characteristics of the non-profit sector to address the issue with particular reference to Non-Profit Institutions. Given the nature and purposes that distinguish this particular type of organized entity, the undeniable difficulty associated with identifying a precise list of elements capable of uniquely qualifying a Non-Profit Institution must be noted. Nevertheless, from the analysis of the main literature on the topic (Hansmann, 1987; Salamon, 1999; Anheier, 2014), it is possible to identify some requirements that are typically found within non-profit organizations:

1. The finalization toward one or more specific public or general purposes;
2. Their private nature, or their subjective extraneousness with respect to the State and its articulations;
3. The non-distribution of profits and assets of the organization;
4. The self-governance capacity of one's own organizational structure; and
5. The voluntariness, which characterizes the participation of the subjects who are part of it.

As already mentioned earlier, the definition just introduced clearly highlights the breadth of the boundaries within which a vast and varied range of organizations qualifying as non-profit could be included and which can be differentiated according to the aims pursued and the type of activity carried out. In fact, this conceptual category includes institutions with social, moral and cultural purposes and whose activities range from those of a cultural, educational and recreational nature, to those typical of the health and environmental sectors, up to social assistance or promotion and development of civil rights, volunteering and many others (Salamon & Anheier, 1996). In other words, non-profit organizations collect within them a far too wide range of social entities characterized by numerous elements of differentiation but sometimes having different points of similarity such as to make it extremely difficult, as already mentioned, a defined and punctual taxonomy of possible elements or distinctive features. Certainly, however, one of the most obvious common features is represented in the provision of activities of various kinds but without any profit-making purpose.

Of course, the absence of a lucrative purpose cannot in any way compromise the previously mentioned institutional approach. Beyond the specific organizational, juridical and purpose specificities of each individual Non-Profit Institution, all organisms inevitably present the typical characteristics of each economic entity. From this perspective, in fact, the sensitive criticalities connected to the definitional issue, mentioned earlier, a delicate aspect to note is represented by the economic characterization of the non-profit institutions which must (or, better, should) necessarily be considered in their economic nature. For non-profit organizations, that is, the same problems arise that can be found for any type of "profit-oriented" organization. Indeed, it could easily be argued, as we will see later, that the social purposes that distinguish this particular sector represent a further element that makes the "economic" management of these bodies even more complex and problematic.

In this sense, just to give an example, it should be considered that the prohibition on distributing the economic results of management which, as just mentioned, is one of the distinctive characteristics of these organizations, should not be interpreted as a technical impossibility of its generation (Salamon & Anheier, 1992a; 1992b; Salamon, 2012). In fact, the economic component in non-profit organizations, although adhering to the structural, organizational and managerial peculiarities typical of the same, is never to be considered of little importance or, worse, irrelevant. It can certainly take on different depths and relevance according to the dimensional characteristics of the individual reality considered, but it is always crucial if these are framed in their correct organizational form which, precisely, remains of an economic type.

In relation to this, then, it should be added that some scholars believe that the composite nature of non-profit companies strongly influences their management, so much so as to hypothesize the ideal decomposition of the latter into two independent macro-areas, although linked from links of mutual complementarity:

- A first area which, aimed at generating income flows, is logically inspired by the operating rules typical of profit-oriented or business-like organizations.
- A second, on the contrary, aimed at the use of the previously created income and, therefore, perfectly compatible with entities not organized in business-like mode.

Of course, it is clear that it is the second management area that concentrates on the main criticalities and difficulties, as the use of the income produced—in non-profit organizations—must be aimed at guaranteeing the correct institutional functioning of the economic structure while respecting the social aims pursued by the same: it is therefore an evident balancing function or reconciliation of almost opposite needs, however fundamental for the company category in question.

The "economic" interpretation of the non-profit sector, however, has not always been so obvious. On the contrary, the social aspect has always monopolized the vision of non-profit entities which, starting from this and combining with the non-profit purpose, has been predominantly and primarily focused on scarce (or worse, nothing) attention toward correct managerial management of an absolutely "economic" organization.

In an alternative way, however, the correct analysis of what was previously reported should be the driving force for the construction of that business vision mentioned previously: it could be said that the correct economic classification of the Non-Profit Institution allows us to have no doubts about the physiological existence of the ability to create economic value in an organizational entity that denies profit only as a pre-eminence or hierarchical priority of its own value system (which is economic). This last and fundamental clarification, on the other hand, allows us to grasp profit in the probably most important and interesting aspect, at least in the economic field: its genesis rather than its (eventual) subsequent distribution.

With regard to the value-creation process, there is an evident and considerable difficulty of interpretation, mainly due to the correct understanding of the concept of generated value. It should be added, then, that this potential takes on substantially different characteristics and meaning in relation to the various organizational forms. In this sense, it would seem quite intuitive to assume that the entrepreneurial form, of the business-like type, postulates fewer pitfalls in the possible measurement of the value generated, as it is directly connected to the contrast between the revenues generated by the activity of transfer of the outputs and the cost-related acquisition of the necessary inputs. This concept has its roots in the economic theory of the conditions of equilibrium of firms, enterprises and for-profit organizations: the survival of these business organizations is ensured by the joint verification of the economic equilibrium (short and long terms) and the financial equilibrium (of competence and cash). The theoretical approach that follows highlights with absolute clarity how the survival of business organizations depends on the achievement of simultaneous and joint balancing conditions relating to the economic, financial and equity aspects. In this perspective, the system of equilibrium conditions would also make it possible to define the boundaries between physiology and pathology of the business system. However, the theory of equilibrium conditions just outlined involves the identification of various limits, especially in relation to the specific context of Non-Profit Institutions, as well as the economic changes which, over time, have shaped the characteristics of the modern economic systems of the various countries of the world. First, the conditions of equilibrium to be guaranteed appear to be purely quantitative. This, therefore, significantly limits its abstractness and, consequently, makes the overall theoretical framework difficult to extend to all the different types and classes of organizations.

Second, and even more for our purposes, the conditions of systemic equilibrium referred to tend to link the ability to create corporate value to the earning capacity and to express it, therefore, in terms of profit: the logical consequence is the tracing of organizational performance to a quantitative indicator that is scarcely explanatory of the process and methods of creating any public value produced.

In this context, it must first be specified that even the conditions for the development of firms are much more complex than the mere maximization of profit which, on the contrary, implies complex assessments regarding the methods of distribution of this surplus among all the subjects who contributed to producing it: in this whole we can find both the owners of financial resources (such as the owner of a business or partners), but also employees, lenders, suppliers, public administrations, as well as the users/customers of an organization economic.

The conclusion of this conceptual approach is the need to overcome the classic vision of profit as an adequate indicator of business development which, on the other hand, is connected to aspects and elements that do not always exactly coincide with the economic and financial wealth of a company or another form of economic organization. This, therefore, also leads to an overall rethinking of the role of businesses and, in general, of all economic organizations in modern economic systems, of their purposes and of the very operating methods that distinguish them. In this sense, the process of creating public value would not represent a typical peculiarity of the business world, but the primary objective of any organization or economic entity.

From this perspective, in fact, it is necessary to specify the "instrumental" or "proxy" character of profit: it certainly represents a possible instrumental purpose of economic organizations, but we cannot at all assert that it is the only one. This is true both for profit-oriented enterprises and for any type of economic organization and leads to two important consequences:

1. The traditional distinction between "non-profit" and "for-profit" cannot be based exclusively on this financial element, but must be traced back to further and more complex evaluation elements.

2. If the absence of a financial surplus (such as profit) is not the only distinctive element for Non-Profit Institutions, then the management methods of Non-Profit Institutions cannot exclude approaches, principles and tools typical of profit-oriented organizations only because of the absence of an element definable as "profit".

2.4 Non-Profit Institution's Main Functions

Organizations belonging to the non-profit sector can be classified according to multiple criteria. A well-known and relevant classification for the purposes of this book is the International Classification of Non-Profit Organizations (ICNPO), proposed by Salamon and Anheier (1996) and reported in Table 2.1. It shows the main functions of Non-Profit Institutions, providing, according to the main types, also some exemplary subcategories.

Table 2.1 International Classification of Non-Profit Organizations (ICNPO)

1	Cultural and artistic activities
2	Sports activities
3	Recreational and socializing activities
4	Primary and secondary education
5	University education
6	Vocational and adult education
7	Research
8	General hospital and rehabilitation services
9	Services for long-term patients
10	Inpatient and non-hospital psychiatric services
11	Other health services
12	Social welfare services (offering real services to the community or categories of people)
13	Emergency assistance services (civil protection and assistance to refugees)
14	Provision of monetary and/or in-kind contributions (services to support individual income and living conditions and charitable services)
15	Protection of the environment
16	Protection of animals
17	Promotion of economic development and social cohesion of the community
18	Protection and development of the housing stock
19	Training, professional start-up and job placement
20	Protection and rights protection services
21	Legal services

(Continued)

Table 2.1 (Continued)

22	Services for organizing the activity of political parties
23	Making philanthropic contributions, promoting volunteering and fundraising activities
24	Promotion of volunteering
25	Activities for economic and humanitarian support abroad
26	Religion and worship activities
27	Protection and promotion of the interests of entrepreneurs and professionals
28	Protection and promotion of workers' interests

Source: Author elaboration.

From what is reported in Table 2.1 it is clear that Non-Profit Institutions are concerned with providing a truly infinite and, moreover, very varied range of activities and functions. In essence, these activities and functions include charity and social welfare, religious, trade organizations, research, education and many others.

Non-Profit Institutions, therefore, are organizations aimed at responding to social problems relating to a certain community and, in the exercise of these activities, can involve people who can perform tasks and duties voluntarily.

This last aspect has also caused some confusion in the names used to refer to the non-profit sector and its institutions: in addition to the non-profit sector, we have the third sector, the voluntary sector, the charity sector, the social sector, the philanthropic sector and many others (Table 2.2).

Table 2.2 Main names used to refer to the Non-Profit Sector

Main names used	*Criterion of analysis*
• Non-profit sector	• *Purpose and objectives pursued*
• Third sector	• *Positioning with respect to other economic actors*
• Voluntary sector	• *Voluntary nature of the subjects*
• Charitable sector	• *Charitable nature of the services and activities carried out*
• Philanthropic sector	• *Altruistic nature of activities*
• Social sector	• *Social impacts, effects and repercussions of functions performed*
• Non-governmental sector	• *Public nature of the mission*

Source: Author elaboration.

References

Anheier, H. K. 2014. *Nonprofit Organizations: Theory, Management, Policy*, second edition. New York: Routledge.

Anheier, H. K. 2000. Managing non-profit organisations: Towards a new approach. *Civil Society Working Paper 1*. London: Centre for Civil Society, LSE.

Arrow, K. J. 1963. Uncertainty and the welfare economics of medical care. *The American Economic Review*, 53(5), 941–973.

Battilana, J., & Lee, M. 2014. Advancing research on hybrid organizing: Insights from the study of social enterprises. *The Academy of Management Annals*, 8(1), 397–441.

Battilana, J., Lee, M., Walker, J., & Dorsey, C. 2012. In search of the hybrid ideal. *Stanford Social Innovation Review*, 10(3), 51–55.

Ben-Ner, A., & Gui, B. (Eds.) 1993. *The Non-Profit Sector in the Mixed Economy*. Ann Arbor: University of Michigan Press.

Billis, D. 2010. *Hybrid Organizations and the Third Sector: Challenges for Practice, Theory and Policy*. Basingstoke: Palgrave Macmillan.

Buchanan, J. 1968. *The Demand and Supply of Public Goods*. Chicago: Rand MacNally.

Civitillo, R. 2016. *L'aziendalità nel volontariato. Il non profit nella provincia di Benevento*. Milano: FrancoAngeli.

Dees, J. G., Emerson, J., & Economy, P. 2001. *Enterprising Nonprofits*. New York: John Wiley & Sons.

DiMaggio, P., & Anheier, H. K. 1990. A sociological conceptualization of the nonprofit organizations and sectors. *Annual Review of Sociology*, 16, 137–159.

Hansmann, H. 1996. *The Ownership of Enterprise*. Cambridge, MA: Harvard University Press.

Hansmann, H. 1987. Economic theories of nonprofit organizations. In Powell, W. W. (Ed.), *The Nonprofit Sector: Research Handbook*. New Haven, CT: Yale University Press.

James, E. 1987. The non-profit sector in comparative perspective. In Powell, W. W. (Ed.), *The Non-Profit Sector: A Research Handbook*. New Haven, CT: Yale University Press.

Moore, M. H. 2000. Managing for value: Organizational strategy in for-profit, nonprofit, and governmental organizations. *Nonprofit and Voluntary Sector Quarterly*, 29(1), 183–204.

Moore, M. H. 1995. *Creating Public Value: Strategic Management in Government*. Cambridge, MA: Harvard University Press.

Musgrave, R. A. 1959. *The Theory of Public Finance*. New York: McGraw Hill.

Najam, A. 1996. Understanding the third sector: Revisiting the prince, the merchant, and the citizen. *Nonprofit Management and Leadership*, 7, 203–219.

Ortmann, A., & Schlesinger, M. 2003. Trust, repute, and the role of nonprofit enterprise. In Anheier, H. K., & Ben-Ner, A. (Eds.), *The Study of the Nonprofit Enterprise: Theory and Approaches*. New York: Kluwer Academic/Plenum Publisher.

Porter, M. E., & Kramer, M. R. 2011. The big idea: Creating shared value. *Harvard Business Review*, 89(1), 2.

Porter, M. E., & Kramer, M. R. 1999. Philanthropy's new agenda: Creating value. *Harvard Business Review*, 77, 121–131.

Putnam, R. D. 2001. *Bowling Alone: The Collapse and Revival of American Community*. New York: Simon and Schuster.

Rose-Ackerman, S. 1996. Altruism, nonprofits, and economic theory. *Journal of Economic Literature*, 34(2), 701–728.

Rosen, H. S. 2004. Public finance. In Rowley, C. K., & Schneider, F. (Eds.), *The Encyclopedia of Public Choice*. Boston: Springer.

Salamon, L. M. (Ed.) 2012. *The State of Nonprofit America*. Washington, DC: Brookings Institution Press.

Salamon, L. M. (Ed.) 1999. *Global Civil Society, Volume One: Dimensions of the Nonprofit Sector*. Baltimore, MD: The Johns Hopkins Center for Civil Society Studies.

Salamon, L. M., & Anheier, H. K. 1996. *The International Classification of Nonprofit Organizations: ICNPO-Revision 1*. Baltimore, MD: Johns Hopkins University Institute for Policy Studies.

Salamon, L. M., & Anheier, H. K. 1992a. In search of the nonprofit sector II: The question of classification. *Voluntas*, 3(3), 267–309.

Salamon, L. M., & Anheier, H. K. 1992b. Toward an understanding of the international nonprofit sector: The John Hopkins comparative nonprofit project. *Nonprofit Management and Leadership*, 2(3), 311–324.

Salamon, L. M., Anheier, H. K., List, R., Toepler, S., Sokolowski, S. W., & Associates 1999. *Global Civil Society: Dimensions of the Non-Profit Sector*. Baltimore, MD: Johns Hopkins University Institute for Policy Studies.

Samuelson, P. A. 1954. The pure theory of public expenditure. *Review of Economics and Statistics*, 11, 387–389.

Smith, S. R. 2010. Nonprofits and public administration reconciling performance management and citizen engagement. *The American Review of Public Administration*, 40(2), 129–152.

Smith, S. R. 2008. The challenge of strengthening nonprofits and civil society. *Public Administration Review*, 68(s1), S132–S145.

Speckbacher, G. 2003. The economics of performance management in nonprofit organizations. *Nonprofit Management & Leadership*, 13(3), 267–281.

Toepler, S., & Anheier, H. K. 2004. Organizational theory and nonprofit management: An overview. In Zimmer, A., & Priller, E. (Eds.), *Future of Civil Society*. Wiesbaden: VS Verlag für Sozialwissenschaften.

3 Non-Profit Institution's Business-Like Approach

Summary

This chapter deals with traditional Non-Profit Institution's analysis approaches, which can also represent two important "dangers" for them.

First, we can clearly note that the need for Non-Profit Institution's managerial techniques inevitably clashes with the absence of traditional for-profit price mechanisms, creating important potential confusions (Moore, 2000), as well as lead to an "overload" of managerial schemes (Skelcher & Smith, 2015). In this sense, non-profit literature has highlighted the need for Non-Profit Institution to be more "business-like": many scholars (Weisbrod, 1991;Austin, 2000;Brinckerhoff, 2000;Frumkin & Andre-Clark, 2000;Moore, 2000;Dart, 2004) essentially make the argument for social entrepreneurship (Emerson & Twersky, 1996) or to employ for-profit tools and strategies to achieve success in non-profit sector (Kearns, 2000), without undermining its distinguishing characteristics.

On the other hand, of course, this could be somewhat dangerous because the adaptation of managerial approaches could have serious organizational and managerial consequences (Speckbacher, 2003;Downe et al., 2010;Kislov, Humphreys & Harvey, 2017).

Second, it must be stressed that the distinction between "profit" and "non-profit" is anything but trivial and, on the contrary, it requires—for the purposes of a correct interpretation—a rigorous clarification of the concept of profit. In many cases, the aforementioned distinction tends to equate the term "non-profit" to the mere denial or rejection of profit or, indeed, to the real abandonment of the typical patterns of economic organizations (Civitillo, 2016).

Nevertheless, we must remember that Non-Profit Institutions are only functionally and structurally responsible for a "non-distribution constraint" principle of monetary values.

All this, therefore, necessarily requires an overall and general rethinking of the concept of profit, which is one of the most relevant conceptual elements with regard to non-profit sector.

3.1 The Performance Management in Non-Profit Institution

As argued by some scholars, performance measurement represents a crucial aspect for any economic organization, regardless of the specific aims pursued (Speckbacher, 2003). This means that the approaches, processes and tools for performance evaluation represent particularly relevant elements not only when the subjects of measurement and evaluation are profit-oriented organizations, such as firms, enterprises, etc. On the contrary, the definition and implementation of performance measurement systems is, therefore, essential for building effective management models for Non-Profit Institution.

Despite what has just been stated, we must necessarily admit that performance represents an element whose measurement and evaluation appear to be characterized by considerable difficulty. However, this is even more true and evident for the non-profit sector.

Defining the concept of "performance" is extremely complex (Ridley & Simon, 1943; Bovaird, 1996; Lapsley & Mitchell, 1996; Atkinson, Waterhouse & Wells, 1997; Streib & Poister, 1999; Kloot & Martin, 2000; Halachmi, 2005). If, in general terms, by performance we mean the ability to achieve results or to respond to needs, it can be conceived in a very different way according to the theoretical approach and the chosen ends (Yuchtman & Seashore, 1967; Ford & Schellenberg, 1982). Without being too specific, we can define performance as an assessment, on the basis of efficiency, effectiveness or social criteria, of the adequacy of an organization and its activities to the expectations of individuals with specific interests (Ricci & Civitillo, 2018).

In other words, performance implies a certain standard of quality (Van Dooren, Bouckaert & Halligan, 2010) which can refer to the quality of the actions performed, or to the quality of what was obtained thanks to those actions.

From the preceding definitions, the fundamental characteristics emerge very clearly (Guthrie & English, 1997; Van Dooren, Bouckaert & Halligan, 2010):

1. Subjectivity,
2. Multidimensionality, and
3. Quality.

Subjectivity is inherent in the relationship of dependence between a certain level of performance with respect to a multitude of elements such as expected results, actors involved, policies, programs and services offered (De Bruijn, 2007; Thomas, 2007): these are elements that present a strong subjective component, resulting in a high degree of ambiguity; moreover, these are factors that could be rather indeterminate, clear and above all constant over time. In essence, these are aspects that make evident the considerable complexity of the performance measurement processes.

The multidimensionality of performance (Moore, 1995; Guthrie & English, 1997; Bouckaert & Halligan, 2008) concerns the need to have a systemic methodological approach, characterized by the integration of differentiated economic and technical variables (Epstein & Birchard, 2000), strategic and operational (Kaplan & Norton, 2001). This multidimensionality can be defined on the basis of its content (width) and its application over time (depth) (Bouckaert & Halligan, 2008).

The breadth of performance concerns the ability to satisfy a wide range of needs which, in turn, is a function of the characteristics of the recipients.

The depth of performance, on the other hand, is inherent in its vertical dimension, specifying the level at which it can be assessed: individual, organizational or general public policy (Talbot, 2005).

Finally, the "quality" of the actions and results achieved has a double aspect. First of all, the performances can contain activities or actions that are difficult for a precise evaluation: a vaccination campaign, a surgical procedure and a school lesson for children are some examples. The difficulties of measurement and evaluation derive from the fact that the performance is conceptualized as "competence" or "ability" and, therefore, each performance can have a high or low level of quality.

The critical issues illustrated earlier highlight the multiple difficulties in the measurement procedures used for the evaluation of Non-Profit Institution which, in general, are characterized by qualitative elements that are significant for the social nature of their objectives which are, by their very nature, difficult to measure. In fact, due to the multitude of interests involved in the proper functioning of a Non-Profit Institution, the evaluation of the results achieved is so crucial that it involves every actor potentially in contact with it. To ensure accountability (De Bruijn, 2007), the systems used to measure and evaluate performance must be conceptually, theoretically and empirically coherent.

Even considering the subjectivity, multidimensionality and quality elements discussed earlier, what follows is that the evaluation process involves measuring the value generated. In the private sector this is based on market mechanisms, while in the non-profit sector the rules are completely different as we will see in the next paragraphs.

3.2   The Role of "Profit" in Non-Profit Institutions

The question just introduced in the Chapter 2 allows us to grasp at least an opportune reflection on the semantic polyvalence of the term "profit" which, therefore, depending on the specific meaning sought, lends itself to very different considerations and conclusions.

Profit certainly represents a conceptual term characterized by an extreme interdisciplinarity and, therefore, by a wide and varied range of possible defining attempts, each having its own particular significant specificity. This is not the place for an exhaustive and definitive study of the concept of profit; however, in relation to what has been mentioned previously and the purposes of this book, it is sufficient to remember that the concept can be declined:

- With reference to the organizational capacity to create incremental value;
- As the shareholder's economic surplus, in addition to the remuneration related to the entrepreneur's general economic risk.

Moreover, it should be noted that the semantic question just reported does not appear irrelevant at all, given that it is precisely on the term "profit" that the "for-profit" and "non-profit" business dichotomy is based.

All this, therefore, necessarily requires an overall and general rethinking of the concept of profit. First of all, we can affirm that there is no universal and univocal definition of "profit": this term differs profoundly according to the object of the analysis. For example, the Cambridge Dictionary defines this concept as money earned in trade or business for the sale of goods and services, after incurring the costs of producing them (Cambridge Dictionary, 2018)

Alfred Marshall, in his book *Principles of Economics*, defines the concept of "profit" distinguishing it from that of "earning of undertaking" or "management". In this sense, profit would be the difference between income and expenses relating to a business organization, or the difference between the initial and final value of inventories and plants. While subtracting the interest on its capital from the profits of a certain period, at the current rate, we can define the "earning of undertaking" or "management" (Marshall, 1890).

From the two previous definitions it is clear that the traditional distinction between "for-profit" and "non-profit" organizations is based on a very complex and, above all, extremely multifaceted concept: it can therefore be easily understood that the relative distinction cannot be considered at all clear and crystalline, but rather blurred in the perimeters of the two conceptual categories.

What has just been reported allows us to understand both the complexity and the extremely multifaceted nature of profit. This, however, necessarily implies that its possible assumption as a possible measure of performance necessarily requires an assessment of the degree of coherence between it and the peculiar characteristics of the economic organization analyzed as well as, above all, of its aims. In fact, from the aforementioned definitions of profit it is evident that its informative usefulness, although absolutely remarkable and relevant, can be fully expressed only when the object of analysis is represented by profit-oriented organizations. In this sense, some authors have pointed out that, in the business sector, the creation of value (as profit or financial wealth) occurs when customers are willing to pay more for a good or service than it costs for its production. In these cases, profit is an overall indicator suitable for identifying the value generated by a company or enterprise. In fact, obtaining a profit implies that the good or service produced is able to induce a sufficient number of customers to pay the relative price for their appropriate purchase to generate a profit: the positive difference between revenues and costs is precisely the representation of the value generated by the use of the necessary inputs.

However, conversely, when organizations that do not have profit as their main objective are analyzed, the use of profit as a performance evaluation tool is not only not particularly adequate, but it can also lead to misleading and incorrect evaluations (Moore, 2000). This is especially true for Non-Profit Institutions that are not institutionally predisposed for profit but are socially oriented. In these cases, the value generated by these entities cannot and must not be measured by profit but by methods that make it possible to appropriately evaluate the impacts and results of the social activities to which they are institutionally responsible (Dees, 2001).

3.3 The "Business-Like" Behavior: A Possible Solution or a Real Danger?

The considerations illustrated so far highlight that one of the main reasons that would explain the existence of Non-Profit Institution would consist in the so-called "failures" situations (Chapter 2): since the market should best provide pure private goods and services, while Government should be more appropriate with regard to pure public goods and services, the primary role of Non-Profit Institution would be the ability to provide quasi-public goods and services: characteristics, the latter would not be provided by organizations typical of the private market, nor by public organizations.

This makes, therefore, the non-profit sector as a sector able to fill the intermediate space that is created halfway between the market and the Government. However, this traditional view of the non-profit sector also has some dubious implications. In fact, the aforementioned intermediate placement, apparently lacking a specific and autonomous dimension, could generate the idea that its operating principles and, mainly, its governance models should be identified as a combination of tools and criteria typical of the two "extreme" of this hypothetical continuum. This interpretation, however, could lead to many possible confusions, representing a real and concrete danger. From the previous chapters it seems clear that the non-profit sector cannot be represented as the simple intermediate conjugation of two opposite organizational realities. In this sense, the hybridity of Non-Profit Institution (Chapter 2) intends to refer to the evident complexity of the non-profit sector and, therefore, to the need to consider, at the same time, very different structural and functional characteristics. Precisely these aspects, however, determine a marked specificity of Non-Profit Institution, which are not simple organizational mixes, but entities with their own and well-defined logical and conceptual autonomy.

Within these types of scientific discussion, some possible interpretations relating to Non-Profit Institution management have arisen. Some of them, for example, have hypothesized that Non-Profit Institution have ideally been too close to the figure of public organizations, giving excessive weight to their social purposes. For this reason, some scholars (Weisbrod, 1991; Austin, 2000; Brinckerhoff, 2000; Frumkin & Andre-Clark, 2000; Dart, 2004) have begun to emphasize that the non-profit sector, on the contrary, should be more "business-like" oriented, so much so that the success of Non-Profit Institutions would derive from the need for true social entrepreneurship (Emerson & Twersky, 1996) or from the need to employ tools and strategies for profit (Kearns, 2000), although without declining the specific characteristics of that orientation.

In this regard, in fact, it should be noted that, recently, Non-Profit Institutions have become part of a process of "professionalization", through the introduction and implementation of a wide range of tools typically used in business-type organizations (e.g., formalization, budget tools, fund raising, performance management strategies).

However, even this interpretation, although very interesting and suggestive, has some elements that are far from obvious and banal. In particular, a particularly relevant aspect concerns the fact that the introduction of business-like approaches in the non-profit sector could be quite dangerous because the adaptation of managerial approaches could have serious organizational and managerial consequences (Weisbrod, 1998; Dees, Emerson & Economy, 2001; Speckbacher, 2003; Downe et al., 2010; Kislov, Humphreys & Harvey, 2017). In other words, the principles and tools typically employed in the private sector for the management of those organizations or the measurement of their performance are not mechanically transferable to Non-Profit Institutions (Speckbacher, 2003), precisely because of their specificity.

3.4 "Managerial Transplants" in Non-Profit Sector: The Risk of "Reject"

In the perspective just shown in the previous section, we need to highlight that both the legislator and the literature have tried, several times, to compare the private market (and, therefore, for-profit organizations) to the non-profit sector (and to Non-Profit Institutions).

However, the real problem deriving from this discourse is the fact that, up to now, this comparison has translated into real attempts to "transplant" the managerial components typical of for-profit organizations in Non-Profit Institutions. Unfortunately, however, medical science claims that:

> Transplantation is the removal of living, functioning cells, tissues, or organs from the body and then their transfer back into the same body or into a different body.
>
> (Porter, 2018)

Moreover, and above all, considering the numerous risks resulting from transplant operations, a so-called "Pretransplantation Screening" is foreseen in medicine:

> Because transplantation is somewhat risky and donor organs are scarce, potential recipients are screened for factors that may affect the likelihood of success.
>
> (Porter, 2018)

Naturally, the field of investigation of this research book is not the medical one. However, we have used suggestively medical terms to highlight—with due and obvious cognitive and interpretative precautions—that, even in the managerial field, the medical "precautions" should be equally necessary. The core matter, in short, is that it is possible to try to transfer managerial "organs" between different organizations only under two alternative conditions:

a) If the "recipient" organization is typologically identical to the "donor".
b) If the "recipient" organization is of different types, but a Pretransplantation Screening is found a high degree of compatibility such as to avoid or at least minimize the "risk of reject".

In the methodological perspective just mentioned, the observation of the non-profit sector can be interpreted as a sort of "test" able to demonstrate that the risk of rejection is always high in every context, even for Non-Profit Institutions: in this case, the lack of consideration of the evident differences with the characteristics of the business- and profit-oriented organizations generates possible negative externalities that that could irreversibly compromise the aims pursued by these attempted managerial transplants.

In fact, in Non-Profit Institution the adaptation of managerial approaches could have serious organizational and managerial consequences (Speckbacher, 2003; Downe et al., 2010; Bowman, 2011; Kislov, Humphreys & Harvey, 2017) because for-profit approaches, concepts and tools for management or for performance measurement are not easily transferable to Non-Profit Institution (Speckbacher, 2003).

Accordingly, the absence of profit-making in Non-Profit Institution as well as, in general, the lack of a specific financial parameter and measure, leads to an ambiguous evaluation of their performance (Civitillo, 2016). Because, as shown earlier, Non-Profit Institutions are mainly based on everything that is not profit-driven, they are governed by a group of interests and values that appear difficult to express with measures (Chapter 2). Therefore, the achievement of their goals is conditioned by the values pursued within their mission and vision and these values cannot be absolutely neglected.

References

Atkinson, A. A., Waterhouse, J. H., & Wells, R. B. 1997. A stakeholder approach to strategic performance measurement. *Sloan Management Review*, 38(3), 25–37.

Austin, J. 2000. Strategic collaboration between nonprofits and businesses. *Nonprofit and Voluntary Sector Quarterly*, 29(1), 69–97.

Bouckaert, G., & Halligan, J. 2008. *Managing Performance: International Comparison*. London: Routledge.

Bovaird, T. 1996. The political economy of performance measurement. In Halachmi, A., & Bouckaert, G. (Eds.), *Organizational Performance and Measurement in the Public Sector: Toward Service, Efforts and Accomplishment Reporting*. Westport, CT: Quorum Books.

Bowman, W. 2011. *Finance Fundamentals for Nonprofits*. New York: Wiley.

Brinckerhoff, P. 2000. *Social Entrepreneurship: The Art of Mission Based Venture Development*. New York: John Wiley & Sons.

Cambridge Dictionary 2018. *'Profit' Entry*. Cambridge: Cambridge University Press.

Civitillo, R. 2016. *L'aziendalità nel volontariato. Il non profit nella provincia di Benevento*. Milano: FrancoAngeli.

Dart, R. 2004. Being 'business-like' in a nonprofit organization: A grounded and inductive typology. *Nonprofit and Voluntary Sector Quarterly*, 33(2), 290–310.

De Bruijn, H. 2007. *Managing Performance in the Public Sector*. New York: Routledge.

Dees, J. G. 2001. *The Meaning of Social Entrepreneurship*. Retrieved December 12, 2020, from https://web.stanford.edu/class/e145/2007_fall/materials/dees_SE.pdf

Dees, J. G., Emerson, J., & Economy, P. 2001. *Enterprising Nonprofits*. New York: John Wiley & Sons.

Downe, J., Grace, C., Martin, S., & Nutley, S. 2010. Theories of public service improvement: A comparative analysis of local performance assessment frameworks. *Public Management Review*, 12(5), 663–678.

Emerson, J., & Twersky, F. (Eds.) 1996. *New Social Entrepreneurs: The Success, Challenge, and Lessons of Non-Profit Enterprise Creation*. San Francisco, CA: The Roberts Foundation.

Epstein, M. J., & Birchard, B. 2000. *Counting What Counts: Turning Corporate Accountability to Competitive Advantage*. Cambridge, MA: Perseus Books.

Ford, J. D., & Schellenberg, D. A. 1982. Conceptual issues in the assessment of organizational performance. *Academy of Management Review*, 7(1), 49–58.

Frumkin, P., & Andre-Clark, A. 2000. When mission, markets and politics collide: Values and strategy in the nonprofit human services. *Nonprofit and Voluntary Sector Quarterly*, 29(1), 141–163.

Guthrie, J., & English, L. 1997. Performance information and programme evaluation in the Australian public sector. *International Journal of Public Sector Management*, 10(3), 154–164.

Halachmi, A. 2005. Performance measurement is only one way of managing performance. *International Journal of Productivity and Performance Management*, 54(7), 502–516.

Kaplan, R. S., & Norton, D. P. 2001. Strategic performance measurement and management in nonprofit organizations. *Nonprofit Management & Leadership*, 11(3), 87–104.

Kearns, K. 2000. *Private Sector Strategies for Social Sector Success*. San Francisco, CA: Jossey-Bass.

Kislov, R., Humphreys, J., & Harvey, G. 2017. How do managerial techniques evolve over time? The distortion of 'facilitation' in healthcare service improvement. *Public Management Review*, 19(8), 1165–1183.

Kloot, L., & Martin, J. 2000. Strategic performance management: A balanced approach to performance management issues in local government. *Management Accounting Research*, 11(2), 231–251.

Lapsley, I., & Mitchell, F. 1996. *Accounting and Performance Management*. London: Paul Chapman Publishing.

Marshall, A. 1890. *Principles of Economics*, eighth edition. London: MacMillan & Co.

Moore, M. H. 2000. Managing for value: Organizational strategy in for-profit, nonprofit, and governmental organizations. *Nonprofit and Voluntary Sector Quarterly*, 29(1), 183–204.

Moore, M. H. 1995. *Creating Public Value: Strategic Management in Government*. Cambridge, MA: Harvard University Press.

Porter, R. S. (Ed.) 2018. *The Merck Manual of Diagnosis and Therapy*, twenty edition. Kenilworth: Merck & Co. Inc.

Ricci, P., & Civitillo, R. 2018. Italian public administration reform: What are the limits of financial performance measures? In *Outcome-Based Performance Management in the Public Sector*. Cham, Switzerland: Springer International Publishing.

Ridley, C. E., & Simon, H. A. 1943. *Measuring Municipal Activities: A Survey of Suggested Criteria for Appraising Administration*. Chicago: The International City Managers' Association.

Skelcher, C., & Smith, S. R. 2015. Theorizing hybridity: Institutional logics, complex organizations, and actor identities: The case of nonprofits. *Public Administration*, 93(2), 433–448.

Speckbacher, G. 2003. The economics of performance management in nonprofit organizations. *Nonprofit Management & Leadership*, 13(3), 267–281.

Streib, G. D., & Poister, T. H. 1999. Assessing the validity, legitimacy, and functionality of performance measurement systems in municipal governments. *American Review of Public Administration*, 29(2), 107–123.

Talbot, C. 2005. Performance management. In Ferlie, E., Lynn, L. Jr., & Pollitt, C. (Eds.), *The Oxford Handbook of Public Management*. Oxford: Oxford University Press.

Thomas, G. 2007. Why is performance-based accountability so popular in theory and difficult in practice? Paper presented at *World Summit on Public Governance: Improving the Performance of the Public Sector*. Taipei City.

Van Dooren, W., Bouckaert, G., & Halligan, J. 2010. *Performance Management in the Public Sector*. New York: Routledge.

Weisbrod, B. 1998. *To Profit or Not to Profit: The Commercial Transformation of the Nonprofit Section*. Cambridge: Cambridge University Press.

Weisbrod, B. 1991. *The Nonprofit Economy*. Cambridge, MA: Harvard University Press.

Yuchtman, E., & Seashore, S. E. 1967. A system resource approach to organizational effectiveness. *American Sociological Review*, 32, 891–903.

4 Non-Profit Management
Three Key Points

Summary

On the basis of the elements discussed earlier, Chapter 4 tries to condense, in a systematic way, the discourse on managerialism in the non-profit sector into three key points.

First, in Non-Profit Institutions the "non-profit" qualification does not mean that they should not behave according to "economic" principles and methods: it is in this sense that their management is not different from that of profit-oriented organizations.

Second, since profit is a fuzzy and multiform concept, it cannot be assumed as a possible absolute indicator of the capacity to create value of any type of economic organization. This is particularly true for Non-Profit Institutions that are not institutionally set up for profit and leads us to an inevitable question: how can we try to measure efficiency and effectiveness in non-profit sector? The answer is not at all simple, if we consider the complexity of these institutions and, above all, it also presents some solutions that could also give rise to potential paradoxes.

Third, the value expressed by non-profit organizations consists precisely in their ability to support and promote in their communities, their role in promoting and sustaining the commitment of local communities and their citizens. In this regard, we can speak of "civic-engagement objectives" (Smith, 2010) which are characterized by high levels of social value and a greater complexity of their measurement. On the other hand, physiological performance objectives also exist in Non-Profit Institutions without compromising the social and civic purposes typical of such organizations. How to combine these two apparently opposing needs? The answer is that even in the non-profit sector there is no trade-off between these two types of objectives, at least if they are governed in a virtuous manner. The element that allows us to reach this harmony could be represented by accountability which, as for any type of economic organization, is capable of improving the overall management of these organizations (Fyffe & Derrick-Mills, 2017;Ricci & Civitillo, 2017,2018) and, on the other, of ensuring even more effectiveness in achieving civic-engagement goals.

The real problem, in this sense, is that the recent "professionalization" process of Non-Profit Institutions, with the implementation of typically business-like tools has led to a clear loss of their sense of belonging and their civic engagement in terms of membership, community focus, citizen participation, staff/client interaction and social citizenship. The final result is a clear decrease in the representativeness and democracy of the Non-Profit Institutions which, in turn, would also determine a certain decline of political favor and engagement of various stakeholders.

4.1 NPI Versus NEI: "Non-Profit Institution" Does Not Mean "Non-Economic Institution"

A particularly important aspect of Non-Profit Institutions concerns the fundamental distinction that exists between the object of the activities carried out and their institutional purposes. As already illustrated in Chapter 2, the absence of the profit-making purpose does not in any way affect the intrinsic characteristics of these organizations which, due to the activities typically provided to citizens, communities and all their other users, are necessarily of an economic nature. This consideration is very important because, especially in the past, it has not been particularly clear, contributing to the emergence of some approaches that seemed to deny that Non-Profit Institutions could be considered as economic organizations. In this sense, beyond the organizational, legal and purpose specificities of each individual entity, the activities by which the Non-Profit Institutions provide the services to their users concern the processes of acquisition of inputs, their transformation and subsequent transfer to a particular group of subjects: it is evident that these are activities of an economic nature as they are completely similar to those carried out also by profit-oriented private companies. The fact that these activities are carried out for profit in the latter cannot affect the economic nature of the activities. From this point of view, in fact, of the delicate criticalities connected to the definitional issue, mentioned previously, a delicate aspect to be noted is represented by the economic characterization of non-profit institutions which must (or rather should) necessarily be considered in their economic nature.

These considerations take on enormous importance because if we admit the economic nature of the non-profit sector, then we must necessarily deduce that even for Non-Profit Institutions the same problems arise that can be found for any type of "profit-oriented" organization. Indeed, it could easily be argued, as we will see later, that the social purposes that distinguish this particular business sector represent a further element that makes the "economic" management of these entities even more complex and problematic.

The non-economic view of Non-Profit Institutions derives from the wrong interpretation of the non-distribution constraint which, unfortunately, has led to some interpretations which, especially in the past, considered the prohibition to distribute any surplus value of the management of Non-Profit Institutions as a prohibition also on their creation. In short, it was believed that the fact that such operating surplus could not be distributed implied that in the Non-Profit Institutions it should never occur that the revenues could be quantitatively higher than the costs. Naturally, this conclusion is absolutely wrong since the aforementioned non-distribution constraint represents only the management constraint that prevents the distribution of the management surplus which, considering the social aims of the non-profit sector, must be devolved to guarantee the most effective achievement of the objectives of the Non-Profit Institutions and not distributed among its subjects (Salamon & Anheier, 1992; Anheier, 2014). What has just been said, in fact, underlines that the economic component in Non-Profit Institutions, while being specific to the structural, organizational and management peculiarities of the same, is never to be considered of little importance or, worse, irrelevant. It can certainly take on different depths and relevance depending on the dimensional characteristics of the individual reality considered, but it is always decisive if these are framed in their correct organizational form which, in fact, remains of an economic type.

4.2 Discovering Efficiency and Effectiveness in the Non-Profit Sector: A Possible Paradox?

In Chapter 3, we have seen that some theories have recently spread that seem to criticize the way Non-Profit Institutions are managed, in the sense of considering them too far from those typical of the for-profit sector. Some authors (Weisbrod, 1991; Austin, 2000; Brinckerhoff, 2000; Frumkin & Andre-Clark, 2000; Dart, 2004), in particular, have begun to highlight that the fact that the consideration of social purposes typical of the non-profit sector we have moved the Non-Profit Institutions away from satisfactory levels of efficiency and effectiveness of their management. In reality, as highlighted in the initial section of this chapter, Non-Profit Institutions constitute "economic" organizations, since the pursuit of typical social goals does not imply that the activities necessary to achieve them do not have an "economic" character: a production process that begins with the acquisition of inputs proceeds with their transformation and ends with the supply of goods and services to particular groups of subjects.

Precisely in this sense, we have previously emphasized that the non-profit sector, on the contrary, should be more oriented toward "business-like", so much so that we can talk about social entrepreneurship (Emerson & Twersky, 1996) or the need to use tools and strategies typically employed to achieve profit (Kearns, 2000).

Nonetheless, it is also necessary to highlight that the "business-like" approaches of the non-profit sector have also been criticized by some scientific studies and research. More specifically, some scholars (Porter & Kramer, 1999; Dees, 2001; Putnam, 2001; Tenbensel, Dwyer & Lavoie, 2014), without denying the need for Non-Profit Institutions to ensure high levels of efficiency and effectiveness of their management, they argued that the non-profit sector nevertheless remains a particular area of economic organizations as the value expressed would be primarily to be found in its role of supporting, promoting and supporting the commitment of local communities and their citizens.

In this way, some studies have spread that try to infer almost the opposite of what is claimed by business-like approaches: it would not be the Non-Profit Institutions that would have to import the approaches, principles, tools and methods of management of the for-profit organizations, but just the opposite.

Peter Drucker, for example, already in 1989, with his book "What Business Can Learn from Non-Profit Organizations" clearly highlighted the potential of the non-profit sector, arguing that Non-Profit Institutions are able to generate new community bonds, and constitute a commitment to active citizenship, to social responsibility, to the construction of global value.

Other researches (Porter & Kramer, 1999; Wondolleck & Yaffee, 2000; Smith, 2008) have shown that the non-profit sector is able to generate indisputable advantages in terms of social value production, such as the creation of networks for the exchange of information for citizens and local communities.

In this regard, we can speak of "civic-engagement objectives" (Smith, 2010) which are characterized by (Figure 4.1):

- High levels of social value,
- A greater complexity of their measurement.

The graph shown in Figure 4.1 highlights that the typical aims and objectives of Non-Profit Institutions can be characterized by very different characteristics in terms of:

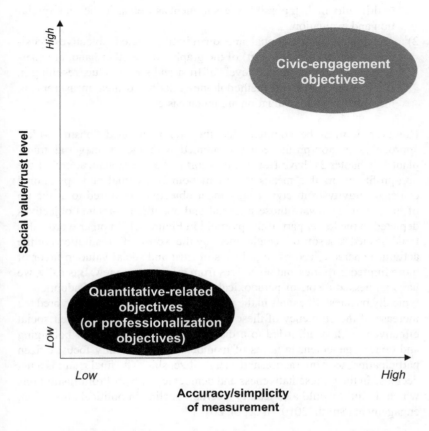

Figure 4.1 Civic-engagement and quantitative-related objectives in Non-Profit Institutions

Source: Author elaboration.

a) Accuracy and simplicity of the methods and tools for their measurement, and
b) Social value or trust level that distinguishes them.

In this perspective:

1) The civic-engagement objectives (positioned in the upper/right part of the graph) are undoubtedly characterized by high levels of social value but, at the same time, they are also those that require a high complexity

or difficulty in their possible measurement as well as in their interpretation and evaluation.

2) The financial, operational and quantitative-related objectives (positioned in the lower/left part) of the graph, on the other hand, are characterized by more limited levels of trust and social value, resulting in that the processes and methodologies relating to their measurement, interpretation and evaluation are much easier.

However, it must be admitted that the aforementioned "business-like" approaches in non-profit sector, combined with the "managerial transplants" (Chapter 3), have resulted in a sort of "professionalization" of the non-profit sector: this means a shift of both conceptual and operational center of gravity from civic-engagement objectives (referred to at the tip of the pyramid) toward those financial and quantitative-related objectives depicted in the lower part of the pyramid in Figure 4.1. In other words, this trend has led to a sort of abandonment by the Non-Profit Institutions of the activities characterized by high levels of trust and social value in favor of more limited activities and objectives from this point of view. Basically, we have witnessed a sort of paradoxical effect: theoretically, the adoption of typically business-like tools in the non-profit sector should have favored the increase of the efficiency of these organizations or, at least, of their social effectiveness. Instead, it led to a distinct loss of their sense of belonging and civic engagement in terms of membership, community focus, citizen participation, user interaction and social citizenship. The final result is a net decrease in the representativeness and democracy of Non-Profit Institutions which, in turn, would also lead to a certain decline in political and citizen engagement (Smith, 2010; Skocpol, 2013).

4.3 The Potential of "Accountability" in the Non-Profit Institutions

What has just been mentioned seems to raise a really important question, especially for the purposes of this book: a sort of trade-off between two apparently opposing concepts: performance objectives and civic-engagement objectives in Non-Profit Institutions. In fact, the attempts to introduce business-oriented logic in the non-profit sector (Chapter 3) seem to weaken the traditional social vision of Non-Profit Institutions, inducing such organizations to a greater commitment in the discovery of management efficiency and effectiveness rather than that for the achievement of civic-engagement goals.

However, the distinctive characteristics of the non-profit sector seem to highlight an element that may be able to link the two extremes just mentioned: it is accountability which, in this perspective, does not represent an obstacle to the performance objectives of the Non-Profit Institution but, on the contrary, a process that is able, on the one hand, to improve the overall management of these organizations (Fyffe & Derrick-Mills, 2017; Ricci & Civitillo, 2017, 2018) and, on the other, to more effectively achieve civic-engagement goals.

The term "accountability" implies the duty to act responsibly and to be accountable to others for one's actions, in order to maintain effective and logical links between planning, decision, action and verification (Ricci, 2016).

In other words, accountability refers to the need to make the use of financial and non-financial resources transparent, but also to the correctness of management skills, the adequacy and compliance between actions and objectives and the clear reporting of the results achieved by the organization (Rosenfield, 1974; Dubnick, 2011; Mulgan, 2000; Messner, 2009; Bovens, 2010; Bebbington et al., 2014; Ricci, 2019).

The role that accountability is able to express in Non-Profit Institutions is evident if we consider that the absence of a profit orientation necessarily requires the measurement of performance and responsibility. In this sense, any possible evaluation or judgment on the mission and activities of the Non-Profit Institutions is independent of the availability of information on their performance. This type of evaluation is fundamental to protect public trust which, otherwise, is destined to be lost (Speckbacher, 2003).

In this perspective, it can be asserted that performance measurement systems do not represent a mere management control tool, but an important element of a much broader strategic approach: all this is proven by the growing focus on both performance measurement and on accountability methodologies in the non-profit sector (Rossi & Freeman, 1989; Alie & Seila, 1997; Hunter & Koopmans, 2006; Boris & Kopczynski Winkler, 2013; Ceptureanu et al., 2018).

The need for accountability for Non-Profit Institutions (Arenas, Lozano & Albareda, 2009; Baur & Palazzo, 2011; Rademacher & Remus, 2017) was also demonstrated by some scandals that have upset this sector and have highlighted a real crisis of responsibility (LeRoux & Wright, 2010). The United Way, Nature Conservancy and American Red Cross cases (Jeavons, 1994; Fleishman, 1999) have highlighted the need for transparent information demonstrating the actual results (Benjamin & Misra, 2006) produced by any organization. This is especially true of Non-Profit Institutions, as Porter and Kramer (1999) argue.

Of course, it is also necessary to specify that, although the measurement of performance and accountability are physiologically linked, they are substantially different, starting with the aims pursued:

a) Performance measurement systems are aimed at understanding the results achieved by an organization, according to one or more evaluation criteria which, however, are generally quantitative.

b)   Accountability, on the other hand, implies complete and transparent disclosure mainly of a non-financial type, based on the different social dimensions (environment, gender, territory, etc.).

(Civitillo, 2016)

With reference to the non-profit sector, therefore, accountability first of all expresses the need to report, in a transparent and widespread manner, nonfinancial information (Behn, 2001) which complements traditional accounting and, therefore, financial information.

Consequently, accountability makes it possible to obtain a sort of "integrated information" (Rademacher & Remus, 2017) able to demonstrate the real use of money in the organization and which services and benefits are actually produced: this is an aspect of provision importance to ensure knowledge of the public value generated by Non-Profit Institutions (Moore, 1995; Esposito & Ricci, 2015).

Very often the concept of accountability that we mentioned earlier is superimposed on that of Corporate Social Responsibility (CSR). In reality, these are concepts that, although closely related to each other, are not completely superimposable and interchangeable (Krisch & Grabner-Kräuter, 2017). Indeed, it could happen that they are even completely disjoint. In fact, the fact that an organization adopts an effective system of accountability toward stakeholders does not necessarily imply that it is also socially responsible. This is because a communication that can be defined as "accountable" may not automatically and mechanically translate into the effective respect by that organization of the possible commitments and social duties to which it would be subject (Ricci & Esposito, 2017).

In any case, the issues of accountability and social responsibility recall that of the purposes attributable to economic organizations and, therefore, also to Non-Profit Institutions. Indeed, we must remember that the exercise of any organized economic activity tends to generate different types of legal obligations. However, traditionally we tend to consider that business organizations have only economic purposes, such as profit and wealth. This, however, is not entirely true. In reality, even if we consider a firm, a company or, in any case, a profit-oriented economic organization, we cannot say that it has exclusively economic objectives. As some authors point out (Carroll, 1991; Ricci & Esposito, 2017), these represent only a typology of possible purposes, because profit-oriented organizations, in carrying out the activities that are necessary for the achievement of profit and their own economic objectives, alongside other types of objectives and related responsibilities, such as those of a social, ethical and moral nature.

The fact that economic and other purposes exist in economic organizations at the same time leads to the need to consider logics, approaches and principles also in profit-oriented organizations that make it possible to ensure that the management of these organizations can allow the reconciliation of needs that, due to their nature, they can be quite different and lend themselves to equally different considerations. In this perspective, a concept that can be particularly helpful is the CSR which implies the awareness that any economic activity, in whatever way it is carried out, can lead to very varied results and consequences and that, above all, they are not only of economic nature, but they can involve different aspects of people's lives. In other words, what has just been mentioned highlights that the exercise of an organized economic activity involves much more than simple economic repercussions: the profit, the wealth produced, the profit distributed to shareholders are nothing but examples of elements of a purely economic nature which, although significant, do not totally represent all the possible effects, all the possible repercussions or all the potential liabilities deriving from the activity of a certain organization.

Indeed, the conduct of economic activity involves the consideration that there are specific moral obligations that must be taken into account, which go beyond the laws and regulations in force and which contribute to the achievement of the objectives beyond the interests of a purely financial nature (Ricci & Esposito, 2017).

Of course, as mentioned before, all this is valid for any type of economic organization. In fact, what has just been said about profit-oriented organizations has only served to demonstrate that if it is necessary to consider also non-economic effects in profit-oriented organizations, then this is even more true and even more relevant in economic organizations that do not have profit, starting with the non-profit sector. Thus, it is quite easy to point out that Non-Profit Institutions are characterized by a high degree of social responsibility. Therefore, the need to report and communicate this type of impact in the non-profit sector is as important at least as it happens in other types of organizations. This is true because, as mentioned before, any kind of economic activity determines impacts of an economic type, but also social, environmental, etc. From this perspective, it is evident that Non-Profit Institutions are quite similar to any other organized economic activity: private enterprises, companies and other for-profit entities, on the one hand; central state, municipalities and public administrations on the other. Nonetheless, it is also true that the particular purposes toward which Non-Profit Institutions tend also place them in a particular situation, since they should be characterized by a degree of social responsibility that is certainly higher than the others and that, probably, Non-Profit Institutions should be among economic organizations with the highest levels of accountability and social responsibility. The explanation for this lies in their general institutional purpose of providing high-quality goods and services to particular categories of citizens, in sectors in which neither market organizations nor public organizations are able to do or, in any case, to do with the same effectiveness. This last aspect, however, has not always been so clear in the research and studies on the subject. It is for this reason that, for example, stakeholder theory has always focused almost exclusively on companies or, in any case, on private and profit-oriented economic organizations, arguing that success, in these cases, would derive from the wide range of its stakeholders (Freeman, 1984; Den Hond & De Bakker, 2007). Similarly, research on social responsibility has always favored for-profit institutions (Habisch et al., 2005; Barth & Wolff, 2009; Idowu, Schmidpeter, & Fifka, 2015), while that on Non-Profit Institutions were characterized by a lack of depth (Guthrie, Ball & Farneti, 2010). Only recently, some studies have definitively clarified that CSR is so multifaceted that it cannot focus only on profit-oriented organizations but involves the context of Non-Profit Institutions with great relevance (Rademacher & Remus, 2017). In fact, it is known that Non-Profit Institutions generate goods and services with a high social value (Campbell, 2002) which, very often, are not supplied by the market or by the public administrations since they do not fall within the respective productive fields or strategic advantages: consequently, CSR can be the tool that allows Non-Profit Institutions to make the complex set of their activities transparent and shared in order to achieve the effective creation of social value (Krisch & Grabner-Kräuter, 2017). In this sense, Nardo and Siboni (2018) underlined that CSR is a prerequisite for Non-Profit Institutions because it allows them to demonstrate to stakeholders the effective ability of the organization to pursue the objectives set by its mission.

As described in Chapter 2, Non-Profit Institutions are involved in delivering many and varied community activities, such as development programs, educational programs, outreach and charity activities, religious education, arts exhibitions and many more. These are activities that have a profound impact on the community, above all because, in most cases, they are activities that neither the private market nor the public administration is able or convenient to provide to citizens. However, this very aspect implies an important consideration: the nature of the typical activities of Non-Profit Institutions determines the creation of a close relationship of trust between them and the community. Consequently, if inefficiencies, management problems, scandalous events or in any case situations that undermine the good reputation of Non-Profit Institutions occur, the community could lose trust in these organizations or in the entire non-profit sector: the final result could be a reduction of possible donations and, therefore, the crisis for Non-Profit Institutions that would be unable to carry out their activities due to the lack of sources of income.

However, this causal relationship highlights that only by ensuring high levels of trust, Non-Profit Institutions are able to survive and develop. This last conclusion underlines the enormous importance that social reporting approaches and principles can play in the non-profit sector. The adoption of social responsibility methodologies and tools, such as social relations, becomes of fundamental importance to ensure the non-profit sector the necessary relationship of trust with the community (Bellante et al., 2016).

As mentioned earlier, it is clear that maintaining the trust of the community for the non-profit sector today represents a real imperative, as it allows us to make the management of Non-Profit Institutions more efficient but, above all, to ensure that the behavior of Non-Profit Institutions is compatible with their core values.

References

Alie, R. E., & Seila, J. R. 1997. Who's using evaluation and how: New study gives insight. *Nonprofit World*, 15(5), 40–49.

Anheier, H. K. 2014. *Nonprofit Organizations: Theory, Management, Policy*, second edition. New York: Routledge.

Arenas, D., Lozano, J. M., & Albareda, L. 2009. The role of NGOs in CSR: Mutual perceptions among stakeholders. *Journal of Business Ethics*, 88(1), 175–197.

Austin, J. 2000. Strategic collaboration between nonprofits and businesses. *Nonprofit and Voluntary Sector Quarterly*, 29(1), 69–97.

Barth, R., & Wolff, F. (Eds.) 2009. *Corporate Social Responsibility in Europe: Rhetoric and Realities*. Cheltenham and Northampton: Edward Elgar Publishing.

Baur, D., & Palazzo, G. 2011. The moral legitimacy of NGOs as partners of corporations. *Business Ethics Quarterly*, 21(4), 579–604.

Bebbington, J., Unerman, J., O'Dwyer, B. 2014. *Sustainability accounting and accountability*. Abingdon: Routledge.

Behn, R. D. 2001. *Rethinking Democratic Accountability*. Washington, DC: Brookings Institution Press.

Bellante, G., Berardi, L., Eynaud, P., Nissi, E., & Rea, M. A. 2016. NPO's governance and accountability practices: A comparative analysis between Italy and France. In Marchi, L., Lombardi, R., & Anselmi, L. (Eds.), *Il governo aziendale tra tradizione ed innovazione. Atti convegno Sidrea*. Milano: FrancoAngeli.

Benjamin, L. M., & Misra, K. 2006. Doing good work: Implications of performance accountability for practice in the nonprofit sector. *International Journal of Rural Management*, 2(2), 147–162.

Boris, E. T., & Kopczynski Winkler, M. 2013. The emergence of performance measurement as a complement to evaluation among US foundations. *New Directions for Evaluation*, 137, 69–80.

Bovens, M. 2010. Two Concepts of Accountability: Accountability as a Virtue and as a Mechanism. *West European Politics*, 33(5), 946–967.

Brinckerhoff, P. 2000. *Social Entrepreneurship: The Art of Mission Based Venture Development*. New York: John Wiley & Sons.

Campbell, D. 2002. Outcomes assessment and the paradox of nonprofit accountability. *Nonprofit Management and Leadership*, 12(3), 243–259.

44   *Non-Profit Management*

Carroll, A. B. 1991. The pyramid of corporate social responsibility: Toward the moral management of organizational stakeholders. *Business Horizons*, 34(4), 39–48.

Ceptureanu, S. I., Ceptureanu, E. G., Bogdan, V. L., & Radulescu, V. 2018. Sustainability perceptions in Romanian non-profit organizations: An exploratory study using success factor analysis. *Sustainability*, 10(2), 294.

Civitillo, R. 2016. *L'aziendalità nel volontariato. Il non profit nella provincia di Benevento*. Milano: FrancoAngeli.

Dart, R. 2004. Being 'business-like' in a nonprofit organization: A grounded and inductive typology. *Nonprofit and Voluntary Sector Quarterly*, 33(2), 290–310.

Dees, J. G. 2001. *The Meaning of Social Entrepreneurship*. Retrieved December 12, 2020, from https://web.stanford.edu/class/e145/2007_fall/materials/dees_SE.pdf

Den Hond, F., & De Bakker, F. G. 2007. Ideologically motivated activism: How activist groups influence corporate social change activities. *Academy of Management Review*, 32(3), 901–924.

Dubnick, M. J. 2011. Move over Daniel: We need some 'accountability space'. *Administration & Society*, 43(6), 704–716.

Emerson, J., & Twersky, F. (Eds.) 1996. *New Social Entrepreneurs: The Success, Challenge, and Lessons of Non-Profit Enterprise Creation*. San Francisco, CA: The Roberts Foundation.

Esposito, P., & Ricci, P. 2015. How to turn public (dis)value into new public value? Evidence from Italy. *Public Money & Management*, 35(3), 227–231.

Fleishman, J. L. 1999. Public trust in not-for-profit organizations and the need for regulatory reform. *Philanthropy and the Nonprofit Sector in a Changing America*, 172–197.

Freeman, R. E. 1984. *Strategic Management: A Stakeholder Perspective*. Marshfield, MA: Pitman.

Frumkin, P., & Andre-Clark, A. 2000. When mission, markets and politics collide: Values and strategy in the nonprofit human services. *Nonprofit and Voluntary Sector Quarterly*, 29(1), 141–163.

Fyffe, S. D., & Derrick-Mills, T. 2017. Performance measurement and management. In Boris, E. T., & Steuerle, C. E. (Eds.), *Nonprofits & Government: Collaboration & Conflict*. Washington, DC: The Urban Institute.

Guthrie, J., Ball, A., & Farneti, F. 2010. Advancing sustainable management of public and not for profit organizations. *Public Management Review*, 12(4), 449–459.

Habisch, A., Jonker, J., Wegner, M., & Schmidpeter, R. (Eds.) 2005. *Corporate Social Responsibility Across Europe*. Berlin, Heidelberg and New York: Springer Science & Business Media.

Hunter, D. E., & Koopmans, M. 2006. Calculating program capacity using the concept of active service slot. *Evaluation and Program Planning*, 29(2), 186–192.

Idowu, S. O., Schmidpeter, R., & Fifka, M. S. (Eds.) 2015. *Corporate Social Responsibility in Europe: United in Sustainable Diversity*. Berlin: Springer.

Jeavons, T. H. 1994. Ethics in nonprofit management: Creating a culture of integrity. In Herman R. D. & Associates, *The Jossey-Bass Handbook of Nonprofit Leadership and Management*. San Francisco: Jossey-Bass.

Kearns, K. 2000. *Private sector strategies for social sector success*. San Francisco: Jossey-Bass.

Krisch, U., & Grabner-Kräuter, S. 2017. Insights into the impact of CSR Communication Source on Trust and purchase intention. In *Handbook of Integrated CSR Communication*. Cham, Switzerland: Springer International Publishing.

LeRoux, K., & Wright, N. S. 2010. Does performance measurement improve strategic decision making? Findings from a national survey of nonprofit social service agencies. *Nonprofit and Voluntary Sector Quarterly*, 39(4), 571–587.

Messner, M. 2009. The limits of accountability. *Accounting, Organizations and Society*, 34(8), 918–938.

Moore, M. H. 1995. *Creating Public Value: Strategic Management in Government*. Cambridge, MA: Harvard University Press.

Mulgan, R. 2000. Accountability: An ever-expanding concept?. *Public Administration*, 78(3), 555–573.

Nardo, M. T., & Siboni, B. 2018. Requirements and practices of social reporting in Italian not-for-profit organisations. In Tench, R., Jones, B., & Sun, W. (Eds.), *The Critical State of Corporate Social Responsibility in Europe*. Bingley, UK: Emerald Publishing Limited.

Porter, M. E., & Kramer, M. R. 1999. Philanthropy's new agenda: Creating value. *Harvard Business Review*, 77, 121–131.

Putnam, R. D. 2001. *Bowling Alone: The Collapse and Revival of American Community*. New York: Simon and Schuster.

Rademacher, L., & Remus, N. 2017. Integrated CSR communication of NGOs: The dilemma to communicate and cooperate in CSR project partnerships. In *Handbook of Integrated CSR Communication*. Cham, Switzerland: Springer International Publishing.

Ricci, P. 2016. *Accountability (Entry) in Global Encyclopedia of Public Administration, Public Policy and Governance*, ed. Farazmand, A. Cham, Switzerland: Springer International Publishing.

Ricci, P. 2019. L'accountability Pubblica. In Anselmi L. & Pozzoli S. (Eds.), *Le Aziende Pubbliche. Aspetti di governance, gestione, misurazione, valutazione e rendicontazione*. Milano: FrancoAngeli.

Ricci, P., & Civitillo, R. 2018. Italian public administration reform: What are the limits of financial performance measures? In *Outcome-Based Performance Management in the Public Sector*. Cham, Switzerland: Springer International Publishing.

Ricci, P., & Civitillo, R. 2017. Accountability and third mission in Italian universities. *International Journal of Managerial and Financial Accounting*, 9(3), 201–221.

Ricci, P., & Esposito, P. 2017. Corporate social responsibility. In Farazmand, A. (Ed.), *Global Encyclopedia of Public Administration, Public Policy and Governance*. Cham, Switzerland: Springer International Publishing.

Rosenfield, P. 1974. *Stewardship, Objectives of Financial Statements*. New York, NY: AICPA.

Rossi, P. H., & Freeman, H. E. 1989. *Evaluation: A Systematic Approach*. London: Sage.

Salamon, L. M., & Anheier, H. K. 1992. Toward an understanding of the international nonprofit sector: The John Hopkins comparative nonprofit project. *Nonprofit Management and Leadership*, 2(3), 311–324.

Skocpol, T. 2013. *Diminished Democracy: From Membership to Management in American Civic Life*, vol. 8. Norman: University of Oklahoma Press.

Smith, S. R. 2010. Nonprofits and public administration reconciling performance management and citizen engagement. *The American Review of Public Administration*, 40(2), 129–152.

Smith, S. R. 2008. The challenge of strengthening nonprofits and civil society. *Public Administration Review*, 68(s1), S132–S145.

Speckbacher, G. 2003. The economics of performance management in nonprofit organizations. *Nonprofit Management & Leadership*, 13(3), 267–281.

Tenbensel, T., Dwyer, J., & Lavoie, J. 2014. How not to kill the golden goose: Reconceptualizing accountability environments of third-sector organizations. *Public Management Review*, 16(7), 925–944.

Weisbrod, B. 1991. *The Nonprofit Economy*. Cambridge, MA: Harvard University Press.

Wondolleck, J. M., & Yaffee, S. L. 2000. *Making Collaboration Work: Lessons From Innovation in Natural Resource Management*. Whashington, D.C.: Island Press.

5 Recent Evolution Paths of the Non-Profit Sector

Attempts for Legislative Reforms

Summary

The chapter illustrates some recent developments that have affected the non-profit sector. Indeed, the aim of this section is to highlight the attempts at legislative reform that have tried to adapt the essential characteristics of Non-Profit Institutions in order to make them more efficient. The chapter illustrates two case studies of legislative reform: Italy and Australia. These are two very interesting examples for the purposes of the book as they highlight very different approaches even if they are aimed at the same sector.

The cases of the reforms of the non-profit sectors in Italy and Australia represent precisely two examples of legislative reform approaches which, although characterized by different methodologies and tools, appear inspired by the common approach of bringing the non-profit sector to the context of profit-oriented organizations. Unfortunately, although the objective of implementing reform processes that lead to an improvement in the effectiveness of Non-Profit Institutions is acceptable, these attempts at convergence can also produce distorted effects. The reasons for this conclusive observation lie precisely in the need to protect the physiological diversity that exists between the two worlds just mentioned that live according to very different rules because they respond to completely different purposes (Putnam, Leonardi, & Nanetti, 1994; Deakin, 1995; Kearns, 2000; Moore, 2000; Powell & Steinberg, 2006; Hoffman, Badiane, & Haigh, 2012; Nardo & Siboni, 2018;). The for-profit sector is based on some fundamental elements, such as the objective of maximizing economic value, the need to guarantee the highest level of financial performance which, in turn, allow us not only to guarantee the survival of companies, businesses and other types of profit-oriented organizations, but also to guarantee their evolution and development: economic, financial, dimensional, strategic, etc. On the other hand, however, the organizations of the non-profit sector are driven by completely different purposes and, therefore, the aforementioned objectives relating to the maximization of economic value and financial performance may have effects that may not be compatible with the social purposes that distinguish the mission of the Non-Profit Institutions.

For this reason, the chapter tries to illustrate, albeit in a very concise manner, the characteristics of the legislative reforms applied in the two countries in order to try to identify useful considerations for tracing potential future development trajectories of the non-profit sector valid in the international context.

5.1   A Comparison Between Two Reform Approaches in Non-Profit Sector: Italy and Australia

In this chapter, we will try to explore the non-profit sector in the light of some legislative reform attempts. In this perspective, it is necessary to premise that the reforms that have had as their object the Non-Profit Institutions are many. The purpose of this book is not to delve into this aspect, but to provide some insight into modern Non-Profit Institution's management. Nevertheless, it seems useful to offer a perspective on this aspect as well. To do this, we have chosen two countries Italy and Australia because their respective reform approaches seem to represent two opposite trends. They represent two examples of legislative reform styles which, although characterized by different methodologies and tools, appear to be inspired by the common approach of leading the non-profit sector into the managerial orbit of the for-profit context, in order to obtain an improvement in effectiveness of Non-Profit Institutions.

5.2   Non-Profit Sector Legislative Reform: The Italian Case

According to the latest official census[1] of the Italian National Institute of Statistics (ISTAT), the non-profit sector in Italy includes 359,574 organizations which, overall, employ 853,476 employees (Italian National Institute of Statistics, 2020). The number of Non-Profit Institutions increased with average annual growth rates substantially constant over time (around 2%) while the increase in employees, equal to 3.9% between 2016 and 2017, stood at 1.0% in the two-year period 2017–2018. Compared to all industrial and service companies, the incidence of Non-Profit Institutions continues to increase, going from 5.8% in 2001 to 8.2% in 2018, unlike the weight of employees which remains almost stable (6.9%).

In the last survey period, the Italian Non-Profit Institutions showing the highest increase are those active in the sectors of rights protection and political activity (+9.9%), social assistance and civil protection (+4.1%), philanthropy and promotion of volunteering (+3.9%) and trade union relations and interest representation (+3.7%).

The distribution of Italian Non-Profit Institutions by economic activity remains almost unchanged over the most recent years, with the culture, sport and recreation sector which brings together almost two-thirds of the units (64.4%), followed by those of social assistance and civil protection (9.3 %), trade union relations and interest representation (6.5%), religion (4.7%), education and research (3.9%) and health care (3.5%).

From a legislative point of view, the Italian non-profit sector has recently been the recipient of an important regulatory reform. This path begins in 2016, with law no. 106/2016 which establishes the basic principles of a matter, however leaving the definition of the details on the concrete application of these principles to the implementing decrees of the Ministry of Labor and Social Policies. In 2017, therefore, five implementing decrees were approved:

- Legislative decree n. 40/2017, about the universal civil service;
- Legislative decree n. 111/2017, about "five per thousand" rule;
- Legislative decree n. 112/2017, about the social enterprise;
- Legislative decree n. 117/2017, about the Third Sector Code (TSC); and
- Presidential Decree 28 July 2017, about the Italian Social Foundation.

Consequently, the current definition of the non-profit sector and its logical-conceptual perimeter derive from the examination of the various organizational forms that have been recognized as such over time. In fact, as just mentioned, the Italian legislative context regarding the non-profit sector has seen the succession of a vast series of rules that have tried to adapt to the changing needs of a sector characterized by high dynamism (Civitillo, 2016). In this sense, in addition to the Italian Civil Code, the following rules must be remembered about Italian Non-Profit legislation:

- Law n. 266/1991, for voluntary organizations;
- The Legislative Decree n. 460/1997, for non-governmental organizations, for amateur sports associations for non-profit organizations;
- Law n. 383/2000, for social promotion associations.

This progression finds one of its most relevant goals in the aforementioned Legislative Decree n. 117/2017 which introduces the TSC with the aim of systematically reorganizing all organizations operating in the sector which, from this moment on, are defined as Third Sector Entities (TSEs).

The innovative scope of the 2017 regulatory reform is very broad and does not end with the simple new name of the Italian Non-Profit Institutions. In this sense, it provides:

a. The provision of the TSC (with the Legislative Decree n. 117/2017), aimed at containing all the rules concerning TSEs;

b.   A single legal profile for all TSEs, regardless of the type of organization; and

c.   The establishment of the Single National Register of the Third Sector (RUNTS, in Italian).

The establishment of the TSC responds to the specific purpose of completely reorganizing the discipline regarding TSEs in order to support citizens and communities to pursue the common good, to raise the levels of active citizenship, cohesion and social protection, favoring the participation, inclusion and full development of the person, to enhance the potential for growth and employment, in implementation of the Constitution.

For this reason, according to the new legislation, TSEs can be defined as organizations that exercise, on an exclusive or principal basis, one or more activities of general interest in the form of voluntary action or free provision of money, goods or services, or of mutuality or production or exchange of goods or services. In other words, TSEs are non-profit organizations, which carry out activities of general interest, or aimed at achieving civic, solidarity and social utility purposes.

The law defines activities of general interest as those having as their object:

a)   Social interventions and services;
b)   Interventions and health services;
c)   Social and health services;
d)   Education, instruction and vocational training, as well as cultural activities of social interest with an educational purpose;
e)   Interventions and services aimed at safeguarding and improvement of environmental conditions and the wise and rational use of natural resources, with exclusion of the professional activity of collection and recycling of urban, special and hazardous waste;
f)   Interventions for the protection and enhancement of cultural heritage and the landscape;
g)   University and post-university training;
h)   Scientific research of particular social interest;
i)   Organization and management of cultural, artistic or recreational activities of social interest, including activities, including editorial, promotion and dissemination of the culture and practice of volunteering and the same activities of general interest;
j)   Sound broadcasting of a community nature;
k)   Organization and management of tourist activities of social, cultural or religious interest;

l)   Extra-school training, aimed at prevention of early school leaving and academic and educational success, to the prevention of bullying and the fight against educational poverty;

m) Instrumental services to TSEs;

n)   Development cooperation;

o)   Commercial, production, education and information, promotion activities carried out in the context of or in favor of fair-trade supply chains, in order to allow the workers to lead a free and dignified existence, and to respect trade union rights, as well as to commit to the fight against child labor;

p)   Services aimed at insertion or reintegration into the labor market for workers and disadvantaged people;

q)   Housing and other temporary residential activities aimed at satisfying social, health, cultural and training needs or working;

r)   Humanitarian reception and social integration of migrants;

s)   Social agriculture;

t)   Organization and management of sports activities amateur;

u)   Charity, distance support, free transfer of food or products or provision of money, goods or services in support of disadvantaged people or activities of general interest;

v)   Promotion of the culture of legality, of peace between peoples, nonviolence and unarmed defense;

w) Promotion and protection of human, civil, social and political rights, as well as the rights of consumers and users of activities of general interest;

x)   Care of international adoption procedures;

y)   Civil protection; and

z)   Requalification of unused public assets or assets confiscated from organized crime.

Although this definition of TSE is particularly broad, it entails a series of obligations including:

•   The obligation to register for the Single National Register of the Third Sector (RUNTS);

•   The use of the mandatory name TSE in any communication or deed of a public nature;

•   The keeping of accounting records and drafting of the financial statements;

•   The preparation of the social report;

•   The keeping of the documentation required by law that can be viewed by all members;

- The prohibition of direct and indirect distribution of profits or revenues or income;
- That must be reinvested for the performance of statutory activities, in pursuit of the purposes of social utility or solidarity; and
- The devolution of assets in the event of dissolution to other TSEs or, in the absence of it, to the Italian Social Foundation, a structure with the aim of supporting funding paths for the Italian social sector.

The new regulatory framework provides for a precise classification of the types of organizations that can be considered TSEs:

a) Voluntary organizations (ODV, in Italian);
b) Social promotion associations (APS, in Italian);
c) Philanthropic organizations;
d) Social enterprises, including social cooperatives;
e) Associative networks;
f) Mutual aid societies (SOMS, in Italian); and
g) Other types of associations, foundations and other private entities, other than companies, set up for the non-profit pursuit of civic, solidarity and social utility purposes.

On the contrary, according to the new legislation, these are not TSEs:

- Public administrations;
- Political formations and associations;
- Trade unions;
- Professional associations, and associations representing economic categories;
- Employer associations; and
- Entities subject to management and coordination or controlled by the aforementioned entities, with some specific exceptions.

Further innovations introduced by the TSC are:

- The introduction of the National Council of the Third Sector (NCTS);
- The introduction of the National Control Board (NCB);
- The provision, once the RUNTS is operational, of a simplified procedure for the recognition of the legal personality of TSEs;
- The revision, reorganization and more synergistic use of the financial resources provided for by the previous legislation in favor of certain types of entities and those of the new financial instruments established by the TSC; and
- The revision of the tax legislation applicable to each type of entity.

Based on what has been mentioned previously, the RUNTS consist of the following sections:

a)   Voluntary organizations;
b)   Associations for social promotion;
c)   Philanthropic organizations;
d)   Social enterprises, including social cooperatives;
e)   Membership networks;
f)   Mutual Aid Society; and
g)   Other TSEs.

To avoid any opportunistic behavior of the Non-Profit Institutions, no organization can be simultaneously registered in two or more sections of this register.

Furthermore, all essential information relating to the Non-Profit Institutions must be entered in the RUNTS, such as the name of the organization, the legal form, the registered office, the date of incorporation, the object of the general interest activity carried out, the tax code or the VAT number, the minimum assets, the subjects who have the legal representation of the entity and those who hold corporate offices with indication of powers and limitations.

The register must also include the amendments to the articles of association, the resolutions for transformation, merger, demerger, dissolution, extinction, liquidation and cancellation and all provisions relating to the Non-Profit Institution.

Finally, one of the most important aspects concerns the fact that, in order to analyze and evaluate the social impact of the activities carried out by the TSEs, the TSC has the obligation to draw up the social report, according to guidelines adopted by the decree of the Ministry of Labor and Social Policies, for all TSEs that have revenues or income exceeding 1 million euros. In addition, the social report must also be filed with the RUNTS and published on its website.

Furthermore, to ensure adequate levels of financial transparency, TSEs with revenues, annuities or income in any case denominated in excess of 100,000 euros per year must in any case publish annually and keep updated on their website, or on the website of the association network to which they belong, any emoluments, fees or considerations attributed to managers and members of the administration and control bodies for any reason.

Concluding this brief examination of the non-profit sector in Italy, it is first of all necessary to underline that it has reached a particularly relevant dimension both if we consider its overall size (number of organizations, functions and objectives pursued, quantity and variety of goods and services offered, etc.), and if we analyze its importance for the community (quality of the goods and services offered, innovative capacity, occupational relevance, etc.). Furthermore, this relevance tends to grow systematically, considering the evident expansion of the needs destined for citizens who:

- Private for-profit companies have no interest in satisfying, in consideration of the low profit margins); and
- Public administrations cannot provide an adequate response due to the limited resources and organizational skills available to them.

It is for these and other similar reasons that the reform of the non-profit sector in Italy takes place in a particularly delicate temporal context, characterized by a situation of profound economic crisis, as well as high unemployment.

The reform is based on the recognition of the non-profit sector for the Italian socioeconomic context: the Non-Profit Institutions in Italy are able to contribute to relaunching and improving the national welfare system as a whole, as well as the country's employment status.

As seen earlier, to implement this reform, the approach followed by the Italian legislator was focused on the economic–productive development of Non-Profit Institutions, trying—on the one hand—to reduce the limits to which they were typically subjected in the past and—on the other hand— guaranteeing them the possibility of carrying out activities of a productive nature in a continuous and professional way (with qualified employees), alongside or in place of the typical and classic social purposes. This reform, therefore, has substantially "entrepreneurialized" the non-profit sector, instead of trying to push toward a better definition of the particularities of the various organizations that are part of it.

In this perspective, the initially declared objective of simplifying the management of Non-Profit Institutions has not been achieved at all, considering that many of the innovations actually tend to complicate the management requirements required of these organizations (e.g., reporting, social reports and control bodies).

Consequently, and despite some important positive elements of innovation, it is necessary to highlight that the new Italian legislation on the non-profit sector cannot be considered decisive, above all because it does not yet appear to emphasize the fundamental characteristic of pluralism that characterizes this particular sector: the objectives, the types of activities, the sectors of intervention and the legal forms that the Non-Profit Institutions can take are so diversified as to require legislative interventions that protect this distinction rather than attempting to standardize as the Italian reform of 2017 seems to have done.

5.3 Non-Profit Sector Legislative Reform: The Australian Case

In Australia, charities and non-profit organizations represent very important players in the country, both from a civil society point of view and for the economic impact generated.

The most recent estimates (The Australian Government the Treasury, 2018) highlight a sector made up of approximately 600,000 non-profit organizations from over 48,000 charities, able to represent:

- An economic contribution of approximately 129 billion dollars,
- Employment of about 840,500 full-time paid workers, and
- Approximately 471,700 full-time equivalent workers employed indirectly.

Taken together, the data (The Australian Government the Treasury, 2018) show that the size of the entire sector is roughly equivalent to that of Australian retail, education and training, or the public administration and safety.

In addition, the data also highlights that 3.3 million Australians have volunteered over 328 million unpaid hours per year through this type of organization.

A particularly relevant aspect for the purposes of this book is that this sector derives its sources mainly from services paid by users, as well as sales and membership fees (about 50%). The remainder is made up of public contributions (43%) and donations and legacies (7%).

As regards the functions and services provided by the Australian nonprofit sector, they can be summarized as follows:

- Health;
- Social services;
- Instruction;
- Research;
- Sport and recreation;
- Art and culture, environment;
- Community development;
- Animal welfare;
- Human rights;
- Religious practices;
- Employment and training;
- Accommodation;
- Aging;
- Childcare;
- Disability; and
- Law and advocacy.

The relevance of the non-profit sector in Australia has been highlighted by several researches (Pilcher & Gilchrist, 2018; Cortis et al., 2016; Gilchrist, 2011; Gilchrist & Knight, 2017a, 2017b) and above all by the Australian Government Productivity Commission (Australian Government Productivity Commission, 2010), which has highlighted that this sector contributes about 43 billion dollars to the Gross Domestic Product (GDP) of the whole country. Additionally, Australia's Non-Profit Institutions hold approximately 8% of the national workforce with 4.6 million volunteers, representing an overall salary value of approximately $15 billion (Australian Government Productivity Commission, 2010).

For a correct understanding of non-profit sector dynamics in Australia concerns the recent regulatory and legislative reforms. In fact, the Australian central government has undertaken an intense process of outsourcing of personal services. This has meant that charities and non-profit organizations have begun to compete for services rendered by private sector companies and, above all, has resulted in new and additional needs and challenges for the entire sector. In fact, this new competition between the non-profit sector and the profit-private sector has required Non-Profit Institutions to develop the organizational and managerial skills necessary to be able to successfully compete with organizations that have always been used to being rivals with other competing for-profit companies. In fact, the Non-Profit Institutions which, as mentioned in the previous chapters, are organizations typically accustomed to supplying goods and services for disadvantaged categories of citizens and civil communities, in markets that are not advantageous for for-profit enterprises and, therefore, with characteristics and operating mechanisms very different from those of the competitive sectors.

As a result of the aforementioned outsourcing legislative reforms undertaken by the central Australian state, the most recent studies (Pascoe, 2017) show that Australian Non-Profit Institutions engaged in the provision of personal services have grown, on average, at a faster rate than both for-profit firms and public administrations. This growth has affected many sectors, especially those of education, well-being, disability, housing and health. In July 2016, for example, the Australian Government introduced the National Disability Insurance Scheme (NDIS): it is aimed at ensuring the provision of multiple services to Australian citizens with disabilities, as well as their families, to improve the quality of their social life (The Australian Government the Treasury, 2018).

A further similar program is that aimed at assistance to the elderly where an increasing number of Australian charities and Non-Profit Institutions are involved in providing direct assistance services to the civil community: this is the so-called Committee for Development Cooperation (CDC), a model of provision of varied services to elderly people of Australia.

The two Australian projects just mentioned allow us to highlight that social impact investments make it possible to merge resources and capabilities belonging to three distinct entities: central government, private for-profit sector and non-profit sector. One of the results is that, in a short time, Australia has seen the birth of new and unprecedented forms of fundraising, such as digital crowdfunding, the involvement of external agencies, direct fundraising.

However, another important effect of these dynamics is the affirmation of the Australian Charities and Not-for-profits Commission (ACNC).

The ACNC is the national regulator of charities. It was established in December 2012 and its activity is aimed at the following main objectives:

a) Maintain, protect and strengthen public trust and confidence in the industry;
b) Support and sustain a solid, vibrant, independent and innovative non-profit sector; and
c) Promote the reduction of unnecessary regulatory obligations in the sector.

Among the various activities of the ACNC, we can highlight the creation of a website, the implementation of a portal dedicated to Non-Profit Institutions and, above all, the creation of an online register of the Organizations active in the non-profit sector: the ACNC Register).

The ACNC Register allows the public to search for information about a registered entity, for example, if they want to donate or volunteer. The ACNC Register is freely accessible to the public and is divided into several lists: each list in the Register shows important information about a charity, such as:

• Its purposes,
• The names of the people involved in the management,
• Financial information and accounting documents, and
• Any actions against the entity for failure to comply with legal obligations.

The Registry can be used to check if a charity is registered, or to find information on activities, or even to find charities to donate or volunteer to.

After briefly describing the essential features of the non-profit sector in Australia, we can try to clarify some important aspects. The phase of externalization mentioned earlier has highlighted a strong paradigmatic and ideological change that seems to converge toward a neoliberal economic path, with an increasing attention of the central government toward the free market, also implemented by means of intense processes of privatization and deregulation. At the basis of this transition lies the typical principle of liberal thinking, arguing that citizens should be conceived as real consumers of services. In this perspective, they are free to choose access to the supply of goods and services necessary according to their ability to pay. Consequently, this should have positive effects on the level of the quality of the goods and services provided, since the typical mechanism of a competition regime implies that the success of each of the competitors depends on its ability to respond effectively to the expectations and needs of the competitors' users. From this, therefore, a general process of virtuosity would ensue, capable of raising the overall efficiency of the Australian non-profit sector (Lyons & Dalton, 2011; Kenny et al., 2016).

In short, Australia has tried to pursue a policy aimed at the privatization of social service providers for the civilian community. In this perspective, this has happened through the introduction of contracts with which the central government acts as the purchaser of these services, determining the types and levels of services to be provided to citizens through political planning systems. Then, the same central government provides for the award of these contracts through competitive tendering procedures: this mechanism should entail, as already mentioned before, a virtuous competition between all potential suppliers of such services, including Non-Profit Institutions, which should favor the efficiency and quality of the services themselves. In fact, through the system just seen, the central government holds and exercises financial and managerial control over the organization that wins the supply of those public services (Kettner & Martin, 1994; Lyons, 1995). In fact, as shown, the state acts as a monopsonist, being able to force the offers of the suppliers of these goods and services below the cost of providing the service. In this scenario, only the Non-Profit Institutions would be able to accept similar contracts, being able to compensate this possible negative economic difference with the use of their own financial resources. Conversely, for-profit organizations could participate in such supplies only by reducing certain costs, such as wages, or by targeting only some specific categories of citizens (Deakin, 1996; Dockery & Stromback, 2001; Webster & Harding, 2001; Wright, Marston & McDonald, 2011; Onyx, Cham & Dalton, 2016).

On the other hand, these contracts have enormous repercussions on the management and organizational methods of Non-Profit Institutions, as they are forced to seek the best solutions to ensure their economic survival, as well as their development (Alford & O'Flynn, 2012; Pilcher & Gilchrist, 2018).

In short, we can assert that the reform laws of the Australian non-profit sector have tried to make it more effective, improving some relevant aspects (Pilcher & Gilchrist, 2018), such as:

- Supervision, control and regulation by the central government;
- The level of responsibility of all those involved in the management of the Non-Profit Institutions; and
- The possible organizational transformations of the Non-Profit Institutions.

This approach manifests the clear strategic choice of the Australian central government to incentivize Non-Profit Institutions' procurement processes of public utilities, rather than deal with providing them directly (Wilkins & Gilchrist, 2017).

In conclusion, the concise description of the main features of the non-profit sector in Australia allows us to show some final remarks, useful for the purposes of this book.

First of all, the importance that Non-Profit Institutions assume in the country is evident, both from an economic point of view, and above all in relation to the needs of the civil community. Organizations belonging to the Australian non-profit sector enable the provision of essential goods and services for citizens. However, in this important supply activity, the relationship that exists between Non-Profit Institutions and the Australian central government is particularly relevant: non-profit organizations represent a sort of operational tool with which the central government responds to and satisfies the needs of the civil community. This aspect, on the one hand, determines the evident function of the policy tool of the Non-Profit Institutions, and on the other hand, it greatly affects the managerial and organizational characteristics of the same which, due to the particular financing mechanisms, are characterized by considerable complexity.

Moreover, this complexity also extends to the coordination and control mechanisms, which are essentially centered on the managerial and financial reporting of the organizations themselves (Pilcher & Gilchrist, 2018).

On the contrary, little or nothing is reserved for the distinctive aspects of Non-Profit Institutions, which are forced to compete with for-profit organizations proven in their activity of supplying goods and services, according to neoliberal logic and typical of markets that operate in a purely competitive regime. This aspect greatly conditions the physiognomy of the entire non-profit sector in Australia which, therefore, seems to assume almost the characteristics of any economic operator. The resulting overall approach does not provide for any relevant consideration on the characteristic aspects of the Non-profit Sector, such as the value system, the peculiar mission that distinguishes it, the specific purposes, as well as the need for effective social reporting that allows us to highlight the characteristics of responsibility and transparency that these organizations generally have as their specific distinctive feature. These are particularly delicate aspects in the Non-Profit

Sector, but which do not yet appear to be fully at the center of the reform movements that have taken place in Australia over the years.

Note

1. The latest official census about Non-Profit Sector in Italy prepared by the Italian National Institute of Statistics (ISTAT) is updated as of 31 December 2018 (ISTAT, 2020).

References

Alford, J., & O'Flynn, J. 2012. *Rethinking Public Service Delivery: Managing With External Providers*. London: Macmillan International Higher Education.
Australian Government Productivity Commission (AGPC) 2010. *Contribution of the Not-For-Profit Sector Research Report*. Commonwealth of Australia, Canberra.
The Australian Government the Treasury 2018. *Strengthening for Purpose: Australian Charities and Not-for-Profits Commission Legislation Review*. Report and Recommendations. The Australian Government the Treasury, Canberra.
Civitillo, R. 2016. *L'aziendalità nel volontariato. Il non profit nella provincia di Benevento*. Milano: FrancoAngeli.
Cortis, N., Young, A., Powell, A., Reeve, R., Simnett, R., Ho, K. A., & Ramia, I. 2016. *Australian Charities Report 2015*. University of New South Wales Sydney: Centre for Social Impact.
Deakin, N. 1996. The devils in the detail: Some reflections on contracting for social care by voluntary organizations. *Social Policy & Administration*, 30(1), 20–38.
Deakin, N. 1995. The perils of partnership: The voluntary sector and the state, 1945–1992. In Smith, J. D., Rochester, C., & Hedley, R. (Eds.), *An Introduction to the Voluntary Sector*. London: Routledge.
Dockery, A. M., & Stromback, T. 2001. Devolving public employment services: Preliminary assessment of the Australian experient. *International Labour Review*, 140(4), 429–451.
Gilchrist, D. 2011. Devil's in the detail. *Public Accountant*, 27(4).
Gilchrist, D., & Knight, P. 2017a. *Australia's Disability Services Sector 2017: Report 2: Financial Performance*. Summary of key findings (national benchmarking project). University of Western Australia, Canberra.
Gilchrist, D., & Knight, P. 2017b. Value of the not-for-profit sector 2017. In *An Examination of the Economic Contribution of the Not-for-Profit Human Services Sector in the Northern Territory*. Darwin: University of Western Australia.
Hoffman, A., Badiane, K., & Haigh, N., 2012. Hybrid organizations as agents of positive social change: Bridging the for-profit & non-profit divide. In Golden-Biddle, K., & Dutton, J. (Eds.), *Using a Positive Lens to Explore Social Change and Organizations: Building a Theoretical and Research Foundation*. New York: Routledge, pp. 131–150.
Italian National Institute of Statistics (ISTAT) 2020. *Censimento Permanente delle Istituzioni Non Profit*. ISTAT, Rome.

Kearns, K. 2000. *Private Sector Strategies for Social Sector Success*. San Francisco, CA: Jossey-Bass.

Kenny, S., & Taylor, M. 2016. *Challenging the Third Sector: Global Prospects for Active Citizenship*. Bristol: Policy Press.

Kettner, P. M., & Martin, L. L. 1994. Purchase of service at 20: Are we using it well? *Public Welfare*, 52(3), 14–20.

Lyons, M. 1995. The development of quasi-vouchers in Australia's community services. *Policy & Politics*, 23(2), 127–139.

Lyons, M., & Dalton, B. 2011. Australia: A continuing love affair with the new public management. In Phillips, S. D., & Rathgeb Smith, S. (Eds.), *Governance and Regulation in the Third Sector*. New York: Routledge.

Moore, M. H. 2000. Managing for value: Organizational strategy in for-profit, nonprofit, and governmental organizations. *Nonprofit and Voluntary Sector Quarterly*, 29(1), 183–204.

Nardo, M. T., & Siboni, B. 2018. Requirements and practices of social reporting in Italian not-for-profit organisations. In Tench, R., Jones, B., & Sun, W. (Eds.), *The Critical State of Corporate Social Responsibility in Europe*. Bingley, UK: Emerald Publishing Limited.

Onyx, J., Cham, L., & Dalton, B. 2016. Current trends in Australian nonprofit policy. *Nonprofit Policy Forum*, 7(2), 171–188.

Pascoe, S. 2017. The digital regulator. In McGregor-Lowndes, M., & Wyatt, B. (Eds.), *Regulating Charities: The Inside Story*. New York: Taylor & Francis.

Pilcher, R., & Gilchrist, D. 2018. The intention and the reality: A commentary on the not-for-profit reform agenda in Australia. In Pilcher, R., & Gilchrist, D. (Eds.), *Public Sector Accounting, Accountability and Governance: Globalising the Experiences of Australia and New Zealand*. New York: Routledge.

Powell, W. W., & Steinberg, R. 2006. *The Nonprofit Sector: A Research Handbook*. New Haven, CT: Yale University Press.

Putnam, R. D., Leonardi, R., & Nanetti, R. Y. 1994. *Making Democracy Work: Civic Traditions in Modern Italy*. Princeton, NJ: Princeton University Press.

Webster, E., & Harding, G. 2001. Outsourcing public employment services: The Australian experience. *The Australian Economic Review*, 34(2), 231–242.

Wilkins, P., & Gilchrist, D. 2017. Accountability for the public policy contribution of not-for-profit organizations: Who is accountable to whom, and for what? In Guerrero, R. P., & Wilkins, P. (Eds.), *Doing Public Good?: Private Actors, Evaluation, and Public Value*. Comparative Policy Evaluation Vol. 23. New York: Routledge.

Wright, S., Marston, G., & McDonald, C. 2011. The role of non-profit organizations in the mixed economy of welfare-to-work in the UK and Australia. *Social Policy & Administration*, 45(3), 299–318.

6 Conclusions

Values, Accountability and Managerialism in Non-Profit Institutions

Summary

Because of the extreme complexity of the management of the Non-Profit Institutions, this chapter intends to underline that peculiarities of the Non-Profit Institutions place them in a "gray area" in which it is difficult to clearly understand the relative management dynamics. Moreover, this "gray area" has determined that the problem of the management of Non-Profit Institutions has been tackled by using in non-profit sector of concepts and practices of very different organizations: in some cases, by finding the solution in the methods of managing for-profit institutions; in others, seeing the Non-Profit Institutions as simple extensions of the public administration.

A more in-depth analysis, on the other hand, shows that Non-Profit Institutions require a specific managerial approach that, in addition to taking into account the aforementioned peculiarities, can guarantee the effective improvement of government effectiveness (Boris & Steuerle, 2017) and guaranteeing higher levels of economic development and community satisfaction (Putnam, 2001).

In this sense, the same considerations that, on the one hand, highlight the complexity of the non-profit sector, and on the other, can be useful for identifying the ideal trajectories of a theoretical model of reference for the management of Non-Profit Institutions: its purpose is to outline the trajectories able to develop processes of development of the non-profit sector (at the macroeconomic level) and of the Non-Profit Institutions that are part of it (at the microeconomic level).

6.1 The "Gray Area" of Non-Profit Sector

What was said in the previous chapters allows us to understand the extreme complexity of the non-profit sector and the organizations that are part of it. Today, Non-Profit Institutions probably represent one of the most complex subjects of study in the socioeconomic field (Anheier, 2000, 2014). In fact, in the previous pages we have tried to describe the delicate functions performed daily by the Non-Profit Institutions which, in most cases, are aimed at particular groups of citizens in various difficult situations. Nonetheless, we have also highlighted the considerable difficulties that these entities are called to face.

This allows us to perceive how difficult it can be to identify and build models of organization and management of Non-Profit Institutions that can be considered effective in ensuring not only survival but also development for Non-Profit Institutions. Of course, this goal encounters enormous difficulties considering that non-profit sector organizations cannot rely on those pricing mechanisms that for-profit organizations commonly employ to balance income and expenditure, supply and demand, or goals with their activities (Anheier, 2000; Anheier & Kendall, 2001; Speckbacher, 2003). This aspect creates a huge disparity with Non-Profit Institutions because the absence of the aforementioned tools makes the management of these organizations very difficult, precisely due to the difficulty of identifying models, principles, criteria and tools that can guarantee the satisfactory optimal management of complex entities such as the Non-Profit Institutions.

Market deregulation and the efficiency of private companies are the founding elements of neoliberal movements. Consequently, the maximization of the role of the private sector was counterbalanced by the absolutely complementary role of the other economic actors: the Government, the Public Administration and the non-profit sector (Valentinov, 2012).

In this context, management, professionalization and commercialization of the non-profit sector can be considered as further consequences of the same liberal ideology.

However, it should be remembered that there are several authors who support the negative effects of this behavior for the achievement of the missions, especially in some sectors.

For example, Parton (1998) argues that, in the fields of community care and human services, management and professionalization are often accompanied by formal audits that replace trust:

> once accorded to professionals both by their clients—now users and customers—and the authorities which employ, legitimate and constitute them.
>
> (p. 20)

In the same perspective, Green and Sawyer (2008) believe that the adoption of management methods typical of private companies are not very compatible with the complexity of community assistance services.

On the other hand, the professionalization needs of the Non-Profit Institutions cannot be reconciled even with the dependence of the non-profit sector with respect to the Public Administration, which also translates into a financial dependence on the latter. According to Smith and Lipsky (1993), for example, the dependence of Non-Profit Institutions on public funds has led to their transformation into "vendors" and "agents of the state": the loss of autonomy that derives from them also means the loss of values and civic-engagement objectives that explain their very existence (Clemens, 2006).

In this sense, a second example we provide for a better comprehension of this articulate discourse is non-profit hospitals.

Hospitals are complex, pluralistic, paradoxical, professional organizations (Mintzberg, 1994). Unlike the "machine organization" (Mintzberg, 1994; McDaniel, 2007), in which management is based on essentially rational premises, hospitals are organizations whose concerns extend beyond economic sustainability and focus on social commitment.

Therefore, if the nature of the hospitals is obviously complex, the non-profit hospitals represent even more particular economic organizations, in which the economic, monetary and financial dynamics must live with the social nature of the services provided: this hybrid nature makes the management of these healthcare facilities very challenging and complex. This difficult combination of financial and social aspects has not been well considered in the design of their management models: this social and financial dualism and the plurality of interests have rendered the traditional models of quantitative management of non-profit hospitals (McDaniel, 2007; Pascuci & Meyer, 2013; Meyer, Pascuci & Mamédio, 2016).

In a recent research work, Meyer, Pascuci and Mamédio (2016) argue that non-profit hospitals are institutions that are intimately based on a clear core of values and whose main purpose is to satisfy the needs of users but also those of donors, managers, volunteers and other stakeholders (Oster, 1995; Moore, 2000).

Moreover, March and Sutton (1997) show that the majority of traditional performance indicators used by hospitals—such as Cost-Recovery, Mortality Rate, Bed Turnover, Occupancy Rate, Average Length of Stay, Readmission Rate, Patient-to-Staff Ratio, Patient Wait Time, Operating Margin, etc.—have a quantitative or financial nature: basically, they seem to fail to demonstrate and to report the value generated by hospital organizations.

All this means that the use of machine-like approaches would appear to be absolutely misleading and incorrect in the case of these hybrid organizations.

6.2 "Managerialism" in Non-Profit Sector: What Potential Side Effects?

What has been shown up to now highlights a very complex overall picture, articulated and composed of a wide range of variables and actors.

The heart of the matter is that performance can be correctly defined as a measure of financial compatibility of one or more priorities (public value, social, environmental, etc.). Conversely, when performance is seen as the aim of a Non-Profit Institution, there is the risk that it may not guarantee balanced outcomes and could even result in the destruction of public value (Esposito & Ricci, 2015). This is the risk that Non-Profit Institutions expose themselves to traditional hierarchical forms and tools employed in other sectors: if mainly focused on control systems, on the monitoring of inputs and on the compliance of processes, they could substantially limit the possibility of adequately enhancing their value system, which represents an essential feature of the non-profit sector and its institutions.

As mentioned before, in fact, the real problem is that all attempts to increase efficiency and effectiveness in delivering public services to citizens were dictated by simple "emulative" ideas.

Nevertheless, they have not been able to accurately consider the significant differences that exist between the various economic actors: this has also led to a distorted concept of "managerialism". For example, with reference to the Public Administration, this was modeled on the multidivisional form of leading private-sector corporations, each with a corporate headquarters overseeing various business units, which it controlled through setting and monitoring performance outcomes (Head & Alford, 2015).

The question of "managerialism" allows us to carry out similar considerations also with specific reference to non-profit sector.

From the analysis of Table 6.1 it is possible to identify negative externalities that, evidently, are identical to those highlighted with reference to the organizations of the public sector (business-type managerialism and financialization). In this case, what we can synthetically describe as the professionalization phenomenon of Non-Profit Institutions (e.g., accounting tools, fund raising and performance management instruments), has led to a clear loss of their sense of belonging and their civic engagement in terms of membership, community focus, citizen participation and social citizenship, resulting in a clear decrease in their representativeness and democracy values (Putnam, Leonardi & Nanetti, 1994; Civitillo, 2016; Civitillo, Ricci & Simonetti, 2019): this was clearly highlighted by the previously mentioned example of the non-profit hospitals.

It is possible to further summarize the whole reasoning emphasizing that the analysis of the international literature and the two illustrated examples allows us to demonstrate that the outcomes of the policy design fragmentation (at least in relation to the objectives of this research) tend to coincide in the same logical direction. In short, there is a sort of policy design fragmentation in non-profit sector to induce managerial transplants: the risk of "reject" consists of negative externalities (or negative outcomes) due to complex phenomena which, however, are observed according to limited perspectives, too specific and, conversely, not in a systematic and coordinated way.

In Table 6.1, as mentioned above, there is a literature review of main references on non-profit sector management: the column "Main negative outcome link" tries to indicate the possible negative externalities generated by the policy design fragmentation in the non-profit sector.

Moreover, in this complex scenario it is clear that the role of policy design should be to ensure a careful analysis of the compatibility between "donor" and "recipient" of possible "managerial" transplants: in this sense, policy design—if correctly implemented—could metaphorically represent "pharmacological therapy" for the treatment of these particular "surgical interventions" aimed at avoiding (or at least reducing) the possible cases of "rejection" (that are the negative externalities).

This allows us to emphasize that the concept of managerialism should be correctly represented, considering that—as highlighted previously—it does not mean a simple "transplant" of concepts, methods and techniques borrowed from the business context: in this last perspective, managerialism would be almost similar to an algorithm or, in any case, a mathematical procedure able to always and automatically lead to better results than the starting point. Unfortunately, economic processes do not present these deterministic features, as Norbert Wiener had already highlighted in 1961 (Wiener, 1961).

However, Wiener's main concern arose from the fact that any deterministic approach postulates numerous pitfalls. For example, in the absence of a careful and scrupulous analysis of the implemented algorithm, of the information used, of the complexity and of the propagation of the error in the calculations, the peremptory and categorical character that distinguishes the result of the algorithm becomes substantially irreconcilable. Wiener even hypothesizes potential diabolic and demonic projections of computational science: as a result of such "distortions", the decision-making result may be useless, meaningless or even misleading. It becomes clear, therefore, that modern applications of computational science and algorithms concretize the risk of sacrificing equity for efficiency, or the reliability of judgments for the mere functionality of the apparatus. In this sense, it would be precisely the insurmountable limits of the algorithmic procedures that had to avoid a superstitious increase in the calculation procedures to the rank of veracious oracles. Unfortunately, this would seem to be a further

Table 6.1 Non-Profit Sector reforms and main negative outcome links

Authors	Selected references	Main negative outcome link
Weisbrod (1991)	*Choosing when to use the nonprofit form of institution and when to use another is a social welfare problem. . . . When consumers are poorly informed, however, it is neither efficient nor equitable to reward producers for meeting demands; the lure of profit is counterproductive when sellers are rewarded for providing what consumers purchase mistakenly* (p. 43). . . . *It is difficult to gauge the success of governmental and nonprofit organizations in providing services with hard-to-measure attributes. . . . Since the economic statistical literature largely overlooks this and fails to measure certain outputs, it systematically undervalues the outputs of public and nonprofit providers relative to proprietary-sector outputs. The view that "if a superior performance is desired, then privatization [of publicly owned assets] is the appropriate policy" is a common one. But "superior" performance is a tricky notion when consumers cannot monitor easily outputs that are nevertheless important to them* (pp. 46–47).	**Financialization (predominance of the quantitative-financial dimension)**
Emerson and Twersky (1996)	*While there are exceptions, non-profit business managers usually ignore the market mandates to maintain focus on constantly improving performance. It is not so much a question of whether the business community actually achieves the levels of performance to which it lays claim (critics have wondered whether businesses actually achieve their alleged success rates), but of why so many non-profit managers do not embrace even the most basic concepts of managerial excellence or the non-profit equivalent of a customer orientation upon which such excellence must rest.*	**Business-type managerialism**

(Continued)

Table 6.1 (Continued)

Authors	Selected references	Main negative outcome link
	Perhaps this is because non-profit enterprises have experienced such failure in the past that any degree of success today seems adequate. Regardless, our inability to operate under the same concepts of quality, pursuit of market share, and concern for customer satisfaction (in this case, that of our corporate partner) remains a significant barrier to our success as completely competent managers and suppliers with whom business may enjoy regular, reliable commercial relationships (p. 277).	
Brinckerhoff (2000)	*Does your organization really need business development skills, even though it is a not-for-profit? Absolutely! (p. 2).*	**Business-type managerialism**
Moore (2000)	*In for-profit organizations, this [the value the organization intends to produce] takes the form of financial targets for the organization as a whole, along with a business plan that describes how a company plans to compete in various product and service markets (p. 183).....* *The principal value delivered by the nonprofit sector is the achievement of its social purposes and the satisfaction of the donors' desires to contribute to the cause that the organization embodies...* *. The principal value delivered by the Government sector is the achievement of the politically mandated mission of the organization and the fulfillment of the citizen aspirations that were more or less reliably reflected in that mandate. Importantly, the value of neither nonprofit enterprises nor government bureaucracies is particularly well measured by their financial performance (p. 186).*	**Financialization (predominance of the quantitative-financial dimension)**

	Business-type managerialism
Behn (2001)	*In this spirit, I am defining "new public management paradigm" as the entire collection of tactics and strategies that seek to enhance the performance of the public sector—to improve the ability of government agencies and their nonprofit and for-profit collaborators to produce results (p. 26).*
Dart (2004)	*A plethora of recent publications exhort people in the nonprofit sector to be social entrepreneurs . . . or to implement "private sector strategies for social sector success" . . . The issue of nonprofit organizations becoming more business-like raises many important questions for the academic, practitioner, and public policy communities. Unfortunately, business-like is quite a general term, with few specific referents (p. 290). . . . The basic distinctions between the nonprofit and business-like terms should be clear. From this basic characterization, nonprofit is understood to be organized around an interconnected nest of prosocial and voluntaristic values and goals with few references to the means and structures by which these values are enacted. Business-like activities are generally understood to be those characterized by some blend of profit motivation, the use of managerial and organization design tools developed in for-profit business settings, and broadly framed business thinking to structure and organize activity (p. 294).*

Source: Author elaboration.

consequence of policy design fragmentation as Ernest Alexander (1982) who, in a research, has clearly highlighted the limitation and inadequacy of some studies on the use of artificial intelligence and algorithms for the search for an optimal set of possible solutions (Simon, 1978).

Unfortunately, from the preceding sections of the paper, it would seem that recent reform processes have failed to grasp the multidimensionality typical of complex systems.

Non-Profit Institutions are organizations whose primary purpose is the provision of services to communities and citizens. On the contrary, profit creation does not fall within its scope. Consequently, if the aims are different:

a) The management methods cannot be the same,
b) It is necessary to ensure that the management of these organizations is always directed toward the satisfaction of their "users" (citizens and communities), and
c) It becomes necessary to guarantee a sufficient degree of accountability.

6.3 Conclusions

The topics presented in this book help us understand how complex Non-Profit Institution's management is (Speckbacher, 2003; Christensen & Ebrahim, 2006; Downe et al., 2010; Kislov, Humphreys & Harvey, 2017). As already mentioned earlier, the multiple peculiarities of Non-Profit Institutions place them in a "gray area" whose management dynamics are difficult to be clearly understood. Furthermore, this "gray zone" has determined that the problem of NPI management has been tackled by trying to "transplant" the concepts and practices of organizations very different from them to the non-profit sector: in some cases, as seen, they have tried to find the solution in the methods of management of profit-making institutions, and in others, seeing Non-Profit Institutions as mere extensions of public administration (Chapter 3).

In this book, we have tried to highlight that a more in-depth analysis shows that Non-Profit Institutions require a specific managerial approach which, in addition to taking into account the aforementioned peculiarities, can guarantee the effective improvement of the effectiveness of the Government (Boris & Steuerle, 2017) and ensure greater levels of economic development and community satisfaction (Putnam, 2001).

This is clearly demonstrated by Moore (2000), who explicitly clarifies the specific peculiarities of the non-profit sector with respect to the Public Administration and For-Profit organizations, in terms of value creation. In this case, the main value of the non-profit sector would be represented by the achievement of social objectives as well as ensuring the satisfaction of donors' needs (Oster, 1995).

Therefore, the really crucial point would once again be represented by the need to keep the non-profit sector distinct from other economic sectors, both that relating to the Public Administration, and above all with respect to the for-profit sector. However, the observation of reality would seem to demonstrate, at least in many cases, approaches that try, albeit in very different ways, to go exactly in the opposite direction. In this perspective, the cases of the reforms of the non-profit sectors in Italy and Australia (Chapter 5) represent precisely two examples of legislative reform approaches which, although characterized by different methodologies and tools, appear inspired by the common approach of bringing the non-profit sector to the context of profit-oriented organizations. Unfortunately, although the aim of implementing reform processes that make it possible to obtain an improvement in the levels of effectiveness of Non-Profit Institutions is acceptable, our opinion is that these attempts at convergence produce distorted effects, despite the declared virtuous objectives. The reasons for this conclusive observation lie precisely in the need to protect the physiological diversity that exists between the two worlds just mentioned which, precisely, live according to very different rules precisely because they respond to completely different purposes of the respective economic organizations that are part of them: Non-Profit Institutions, on the one hand, and for-profit organizations, on the other. The for-profit sector stands on the compatibility of some basic elements, such as the objective of maximizing economic value, the need to guarantee the highest level of financial performance. These, in turn, allow us not only to ensure the survival of companies, businesses and other types of profit-oriented organizations, but also to ensure their evolution and development: economic, financial, dimensional, strategic, etc. On the other hand, however, the organizations of the non-profit sector are animated by completely different purposes from the latter and, therefore, the aforementioned goals relating to the maximization of economic value and financial performance may imply effects that may not be compatible with the social purposes that distinguish the mission of the Non-Profit Institutions.

However, it is necessary to underline that what has just been highlighted does not mean that the non-profit sector is not capable of producing value. On the contrary, Non-Profit Institutions can produce very high levels of value, even if not necessarily—and, above all, not exclusively—of an economic-financial nature. As previously shown, the organizations belonging to the non-profit sector produce value through the effective achievement of the social objectives that distinguish their mission (Moore, 2000; Meynhardt, 2009).

However, what has just been highlighted allows one last but very interesting consideration. The aforementioned perspective just represented certainly highlights the complexity of the non-profit sector, as has been stressed several times in this book. On the other hand, however, this complexity is not necessarily to be considered as an element of difficulty: on the contrary, it can even be useful for identifying the ideal trajectories of a theoretical reference model for managing Non-Profit Institutions.

In fact, as represented in this book, it is evident that the non-profit sector must be based on particular and peculiar logics of the social purposes of which it is the interpreter. In summary, we can isolate the following key elements (Figure 6.1):

1. Values

    The non-profit sector is built on a very deep value system (Chapter 2) which necessarily influences its organization, the performance of its organizations and, of course, its goals. Among the typical elements of

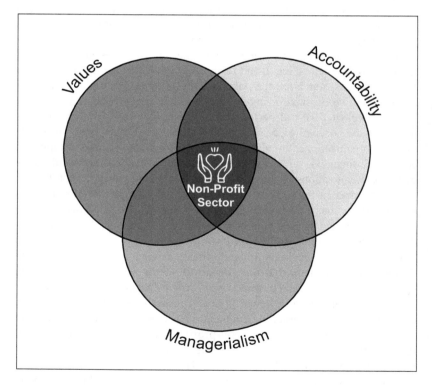

Figure 6.1 Key elements of Non-Profit Sector management

Source: Author elaboration.

this value system, we can find civic engagement, citizen participation, mission, vision, culture, politics, religion, ethics, voluntarism, philanthropy, giving, compassion, civil society, charity, social and relational capital, and many others.

2. Accountability

The purposes, the distinctive characteristics of the non-profit sector, in addition to the aforementioned value system, imply a very high degree of responsibility, which can be declined with reference to a multitude of aspects such as transparency and non-financial disclosure, ethics, learning processes, etc.

3. Managerialism

In Non-Profit Institutions, the absence of a lucrative purpose cannot in any way compromise the previously mentioned characteristics of each economic entity (Chapter 2). Indeed, the social purposes that distinguish this particular sector represent a further element that makes the "economic" management of these bodies even more complex and problematic. In addition, the acquisition of resources (financial and otherwise) in NPI is very sensitive to levels of efficiency and effectiveness in the pursuit of the aforementioned social objectives, with evident management consequences. In this perspective, business-like behavior, performance measurement methodologies, reporting and evaluation tools, efficiency, effectiveness, are typical elements of managerialism which, beyond the possible side effects described earlier (Chapter 6), today represents an element to be valued, albeit without ever compromising the social aims described previously.

The theoretical scheme just described seems to clearly represent the typical approach of co-production. In fact, in the non-profit sector it is essential to involve the civil community in service delivery (Joshi & Moore, 2004).

In this sense, co-production emphasizes a pluralistic model of public service based on a sort of weaving between public, private and nongovernmental actors and would thus be able to guarantee the creation of public value by improving levels of efficiency, effectiveness and innovation (Osborne, Radnor & Nasi, 2013; Nabatchi, Sancino & Sicilia, 2017).

In other words, co-production seems to represent the tools for a renewed public service delivery system in which citizens play an active role for the whole community and for the generation of public value (Ricci & Esposito, 2015), especially in the modern era in which the effects of the global financial crisis make the search for efficiency in the provision of community services an absolute and substantial imperative and not a mere formal option. In other words, we could therefore say that co-creation/ co-production represent, today, for politicians a necessary condition to create innovative public services that effectively meet the needs of citizens within a context characterized by various environmental constraints in which the Non-Profit Institutions operate (Voorberg, Bekkers & Tummers, 2014).

Finally, the three key elements mentioned previously can be read in the light of the concept of Public Value: this could represent an overall and global measure of the whole theorized model.

The literature on public value is exterminated. However, with specific reference to the non-profit sector, it is particularly important to underline that it becomes indispensable to guarantee consent, the rights, benefits and prerogatives of a civil community but also the duties and obligations of every citizen toward society, the State (Bozeman, 2007).

In this sense, public value makes it possible to ensure a systematic approach to the general purpose typical of Non-Profit Institutions: to contribute to improving the overall level of well-being of the community.

References

Alexander, E. R. 1982. Design in the decision-making process. *Policy Sciences*, 14(3), 279–292.

Anheier, H. K. 2014. *Nonprofit Organizations: Theory, Management, Policy*, second edition. New York: Routledge.

Anheier, H. K. 2000. Managing non-profit organisations: Towards a new approach. *Civil Society Working Paper 1*.

Anheier, H. K., & Kendall, J. 2001. *Third Sector Policy at the Crossroad: An International Nonprofit Analysis*. London: Routledge.

Behn, R. D. 2001. *Rethinking Democratic Accountability*. Washington, DC: Brookings Institution Press.

Boris, E. T., & Steuerle, C. E. (Eds.) 2017. *Nonprofits & Government: Collaboration & Conflict*. Washington, DC: The Urban Institute.

Bozeman, B. 2007. *Public Values and Public Interest: Counterbalancing Economic Individualism*. Washington, DC: Georgetown University Press.

Brinckerhoff, P. 2000. *Social Entrepreneurship: The Art of Mission Based Venture Development*. New York: John Wiley & Sons.

Christensen, R. A., & Ebrahim, A. 2006. How does accountability affect mission? The case of a nonprofit serving immigrants and refugees. *Nonprofit Management and Leadership*, 17(2), 195–209.

Civitillo, R. 2016. *L'aziendalità nel volontariato. Il non profit nella provincia di Benevento*. Milano: FrancoAngeli.

Civitillo, R., Ricci, P., & Simonetti, B. 2019. Management and performance of non-profit institutions: Finding new development trajectories-evidence from Italy. *Quality & Quantity*, 53(5), 2275–2290.

Clemens, E. 2006. The constitution of citizens: Political theories of nonprofit organization. In Powell, W. W., & Steinberg, R. (Eds.), *The Nonprofit Sector: A Research Handbook*. New Haven, CT: Yale University Press.

Dart, R. 2004. Being 'business-like' in a nonprofit organization: A grounded and inductive typology. *Nonprofit and Voluntary Sector Quarterly*, 33(2), 290–310.

Downe, J., Grace, C., Martin, S., & Nutley, S. 2010. Theories of public service improvement: A comparative analysis of local performance assessment frameworks. *Public Management Review*, 12(5), 663–678.

Emerson, J., & Twersky, F. (Eds.) 1996. *New Social Entrepreneurs: The Success, Challenge, and Lessons of Non-Profit Enterprise Creation*. San Francisco, CA: The Roberts Foundation.

Esposito, P., & Ricci, P. 2015. How to turn public (dis)value into new public value? Evidence from Italy. *Public Money & Management*, 35(3), 227–231.

Green, D., & Sawyer, A. M. 2008. Risk, regulation, integration: Implications for governance in community service organisations. *Just Policy: A Journal of Australian Social Policy*, 49, 13–22.

Head, B. W., & Alford, J. 2015. Wicked problems: Implications for public policy and management. *Administration & Society*, 47(6), 711–739.

Joshi, A., & Moore, M. 2004. Institutionalised co-production: Unorthodox public service delivery in challenging environments. *Journal of Development Studies*, 40(4), 31–49.

Kislov, R., Humphreys, J., & Harvey, G. 2017. How do managerial techniques evolve over time? The distortion of 'facilitation' in healthcare service improvement. *Public Management Review*, 19(8), 1165–1183.

March, J. G., & Sutton, R. I. 1997. Crossroads-organizational performance as a dependent variable. *Organization Science*, 8(6), 698–706.

McDaniel, R. R. 2007. Management strategies for complex adaptive systems sensemaking, learning, and improvisation. *Performance Improvement Quarterly*, 20(2), 21–41.

Meyer, V., Pascuci, L., & Mamédio, D. F. 2016. Managerialism in complex systems: Experiences of strategic planning in non-profit hospitals. In Pinheiro, R., Geschwind, L., Ramirez, F. O., & VrangbÆk, K. (Eds.), *Towards a Comparative Institutionalism: Forms, Dynamics and Logics Across the Organizational Fields of Health Care and Higher Education*. Bingley: Emerald Group Publishing Limited.

Meynhardt, T. 2009. Public value inside: What is public value creation? *International Journal of Public Administration*, 32(3–4), 192–219.

Moore, M. H. 2000. Managing for value: Organizational strategy in for-profit, nonprofit, and governmental organizations. *Nonprofit and Voluntary Sector Quarterly*, 29(1), 183–204.

Nabatchi, T., Sancino, A., & Sicilia, M. 2017. Varieties of participation in public services: The who, when, and what of coproduction. *Public Administration Review*, 77(5), 766–776.

Osborne, S. P., Radnor, Z., & Nasi, G. 2013. A new theory for public service management? Toward a (public) service-dominant approach. *The American Review of Public Administration*, 43(2), 135–158.

Oster, S. M. 1995. *Strategic Management for Nonprofit Organizations: Theory and Cases*. New York and Oxford: Oxford University Press.

Parton, N. 1998. Risk, advanced liberalism and child welfare: The need to rediscover uncertainty and ambiguity. *The British Journal of Social Work*, 28(1), 5–27.

Pascuci, L., & Meyer, V. Jr. 2013. Estratégia em Contextos Complexos e Pluralísticos. *Revista de Administração Contemporânea*, 17(5), 536–555.

Putnam, R. D. 2001. *Bowling Alone: The Collapse and Revival of American Community*. New York: Simon and Schuster.

Putnam, R. D., Leonardi, R., & Nanetti, R. Y. 1994. *Making Democracy Work: Civic Traditions in Modern Italy*. Princeton, NJ: Princeton University Press.

Ricci, P., & Esposito, P. 2015. How to turn public (dis)value into new public value? Evidence from Italy. *Public Money & Management*, 35(3).

Simon, H. A. 1978. On how to decide what to do. *The Bell Journal of Economics*, 494–507.

Smith, S. R., & Lipsky, M. 1993. *Nonprofits for Hire: The Welfare State in the Age of Contracting*. Cambridge, MA: Harvard University Press.

Speckbacher, G. 2003. The economics of performance management in nonprofit organizations. *Nonprofit Management & Leadership*, 13(3), 267–281.

Valentinov, V. 2012. Toward a critical systems perspective on the nonprofit sector. *Systemic Practice and Action Research*, 25(4), 355–364.

Voorberg, W. H., Bekkers, V. J., & Tummers, L. G. 2014. A systematic review of co-creation and co-production: Embarking on the social innovation journey. *Public Management Review*, 17(9), 1333–1357.

Weisbrod, B. 1991. *The Nonprofit Economy*. Cambridge, MA: Harvard University Press.

Wiener, N. 1961. *Cybernetics or Control and Communication in the Animal and the Machine*. Cambridge and London: MIT Press.

Index

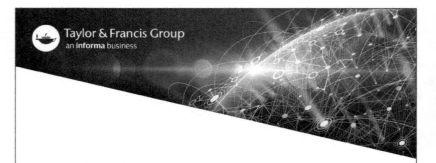